THE SHAKING OF THE
FOUNDATIONS

Also by Paul Tillich

THE NEW BEING

a companion volume to

<small>THE SHAKING</small>

<small>OF THE FOUNDATIONS</small>

Paul Tillich was born in Prussia in 1886. He taught philosophy and theology at the universities of Marburg, Dresden, Leipzig, and Frankfurt. A leader of the Religious Socialist movement, his activities brought him into conflict with Nazism and he was requested to leave Germany in 1933 shortly after Hitler assumed power. From 1933-1955 Dr. Tillich was professor at Union Theological Seminary in New York. He is now University Professor at Harvard.

THE
SHAKING
OF THE
FOUNDATIONS

By

PAUL TILLICH

NEW YORK
CHARLES SCRIBNER'S SONS

To
ERDMUTHE

Preface

THERE ARE two reasons why I agreed to the publication of a book of sermons at this time. Many of my students and friends outside the Seminary have told me of the difficulty they have met in trying to penetrate my theological thought. They believe that through my sermons the practical or, more exactly, the existential implications of my theology are more clearly manifest. I should like to think that the sermons included here help to show that the strictly systematic character of a theology does not need to prevent it from being "practical"—that is to say: applicable to the personal and social problems of our religious life.

There is, however, a more important reason for the publication of this volume. A large part of the congregation at the Sunday services came from outside the Christian circle in the most radical sense of the phrase. For them, a sermon in traditional Biblical terms would have had no meaning. Therefore, I was obliged to seek a language which expresses in other terms the human experience to which the Biblical and ecclesiastical terminology point. In this situation, an "apologetic" type of sermon has been developed. And, since I believe that this is generally the situation in which the Christian message has to be pronounced today, I hope that the publication of some attempts to meet this situation may not be useless.

The sermons in this collection are printed as they were delivered, with only minor changes; I did not rewrite them for publication. Most of them were delivered at Union Theological Seminary, either in the Sunday chapel service or in daily chapel. Only those sermons are included which evoked such a response from the students that the sermons had to be mimeographed.

The Biblical texts are taken from several different translations: the King James, the Moffatt, the Smith and Goodspeed, the Revised Standard Version, and some commentaries. For permission to use the last three versions I am indebted respectively to Harper & Brothers, The University of Chicago Press, and The International Council of Religious Education. In many cases I have combined several different translations to form the text given.

I wish to acknowledge my thanks to *Christendom* for permission to reprint the sermon, "Nature, Also, Mourns for a Lost Good"; to *The Protestant* for permission to reprint "The Escape from God"; and to the *Union Review* for permission to reprint "The Theologian" and "The Two Servants of Jahweh."

The volume could not have been published without the intensive work of several of my former students in revising and organizing the sermons with great understanding and creative criticism. I wish to express my deep thanks to Miss Mary Heilner, Miss Elizabeth Cooper, Miss Caroline Speer, the Reverend William O. Fennell and the Reverend William R. Coleman.

PAUL TILLICH

NEW YORK CITY

Contents

THE SHAKING OF THE
FOUNDATIONS

1

THE SHAKING OF THE FOUNDATIONS

I look out on earth . . . lo, all is chaos;
I look at heaven . . . its light is gone;
I look out on the mountains . . . they are trem-
  bling;
And all the hills are swaying!
I look out . . . lo, no man is to be seen;
All the birds have flown!
I look out . . . lo, the sown land lies a desert;
And the towns are all razed by the Lord's rage.
For thus has the Lord said:
The whole land shall be desolate . . .
And for this shall the earth mourn
And the heavens above be black . . .
I have purposed it and will not repent;
Neither will I turn back from it.
At the noise of the horsemen and the archers
The land is all in flight,
Men taking refuge within woods and caves,
And climbing upon the rocks.
Every city shall be abandoned,
And not a man dwell therein.
You ruined creature, what will you do!
                                JEREMIAH 4:23-30.

For the mountains shall depart,
And the hills be removed.
But my kindness shall not depart from thee;
Neither shall the covenant of my peace be removed,
Saith the Lord that has mercy on thee!

ISAIAH 54:10.

The foundations of the earth do shake.
Earth breaks to pieces,
Earth is split in pieces,
Earth shakes to pieces,
Earth reels like a drunken man,
Earth rocks like a hammock;
Under the weight of its transgression earth falls
*   down*
To rise no more!

Lift up your eyes to heaven and look upon the earth
*   beneath:*
For the heavens shall vanish away like smoke.
And the earth shall grow old like a robe;
The world itself shall crumble.
But my righteousness shall be forever,
And my salvation knows no end.

ISAIAH 24:18-20.

IT IS HARD TO SPEAK AFTER THE prophets have spoken as they have in these pronouncements. Every word is like the stroke of a hammer. There was a time when we could listen to such words without much feeling and without understanding. There were decades and even centuries when we did not take them seriously. Those days are gone. Today we must take them seriously. For they describe with visionary power what the majority of human beings in our period have experienced, and what, perhaps in a not too distant future, all mankind will experience abundantly. "The foundations of the earth do shake." The visions of the prophets have become an actual, physical possibility, and might become an historical reality. The phrase, "Earth is split in pieces," is not merely a poetic metaphor for us, but a hard reality. That is the religious meaning of the age into which we have entered.

The Bible has always told us of the beginning and the end of the world. It speaks of eternity before the world was founded; it speaks of the time when God laid the foundations of the earth; it speaks of the shaking of these foundations and of the crumbling of the world. In one of the later books, Second Peter, it says that "the heavens will vanish with a crackling roar, and the elements will melt with fervent heat, the earth also and the works therein shall be burnt up." This is no longer vision; it has become physics. We know that in the ground of our earth, and in the ground of everything in our world that has form and structure, destructive forces are bound. Laying the foundations of the earth means binding these forces. When the unruly power of the smallest parts of our material world was restrained by cohesive structures, a place was provided in which life could grow and history develop, in which words could be heard and love be felt, and in which truth could be discovered and the Eternal adored. All this was possible because the fiery chaos of the beginning was transformed into the fertile soil of the earth.

But out of the fertile soil of the earth a being was generated and nourished, who was able to find the key to the foundation of all beings. That being was man. He has discovered the key which can unlock the forces of the ground, those forces which were bound when the foundations of the earth were laid. He has begun to use this key. He has subjected the basis of life and thought and will to *his* will. And he willed destruction. For the sake of destruction he used the forces of the ground; by his thought and his work he unlocked and untied them. That is why the foundations of the earth rock and shake in our time.

In the language of the prophets, it is the Lord Who shakes the mountains and melts the rocks. This is a language that modern man can not understand. And so God, Who is not bound to any special language, not even to that of the prophets, spoke to the men of today through the mouths of our greatest scientists, and this is what He said: You yourselves can bring about the end upon yourselves. I give the power to shake the foundations of your earth into your hands. You can use this power for creation or destruction. How will you use it? This is what God said to mankind through the work of the scientists and through their discovery of the key to the foundations of life. But through them He did even more. He forced His Word upon them, as He had forced it upon the prophets, in spite of their attempt ever to resist it. For no prophet likes to say what he has to say. And no scientist who participated in the great and terrible discovery liked to say what he had to say. But he could not but speak; he had to raise his voice, like the prophets, to tell this generation what the prophets told their generations: that earth and man, trees and animals, are threatened by a catastrophe which they can scarcely escape. A tremendous anxiety expresses itself through the words of these men. Not only do they feel the shaking of the foundations, but also that they themselves are largely responsible for it. They tell us that they *despise* what they have done, because they know that we are left with only a slight chance of escape. Wavering between little hope and much despair, they urge us to use this chance.

This is the way in which God had spoken to our generation about the shaking of the foundations. We had forgotten about such shaking. And it was science, more than anything else, which had made us forget it. It was not science as knowledge, but rather science for the purpose of hidden idolatry, for the purpose of persuading us to believe in our earth as the place for the establishment of the Kingdom of God, to believe in ourselves as those through whom this was to be achieved. There were prophets of this idolatry—false prophets, as they were called by Jeremiah—who cried: "Progress, infinite progress! Peace, universal peace! Happiness, happiness for everyone!" And now what has happened? That same science, in the saving power of which these false prophets believed, has utterly destroyed that idolatry. The greatest triumph of science was the power it gave to man to annihilate himself and his world. And those who brought about this triumph are speaking today, like the true prophets of the past—which is to say, not of progress, but of a return to the chaos of the beginning; not of peace, but of disruption; and not of happiness, but of doom. In this way science is atoning for the idolatrous abuse to which it has lent itself for centuries. Science, which has closed our eyes and thrown us into an abyss of ignorance about the few things that really matter, has revealed itself, has opened our eyes, and has pointed, at least, to one fundamental truth—that "the mountains shall depart and the hills shall be removed", that "earth shall fall down to rise no more", because its foundations shall be destroyed.

But still we hear voices—and since the first shock, they have been increasing—which try to comfort us, saying: "Perhaps man will use the power to shake the foundations for creative purposes, for progress, for peace and happiness. The future lies in man's hands, in our hands. If we should decide for constructiveness instead of destruction, why should we not be able to continue the creation? Why should we not become like God, at least in this respect?" Job had to become silent when the Lord spoke to *him* out of the whirlwind, saying, "Where wast thou when I laid the foundations of the earth? Declare if thou hast understanding!" But our false voices continue: "Perhaps *we* can answer where Job could not. Have not our scientific discoveries revealed the mysteries of the ways in which the earth was founded? Are we not, in thought and knowledge, able to be present at this event? Why should we be afraid of the shaking of the foundations?" But man is not God; and whenever he has claimed to be like God, he has been rebuked and brought to self-destruction and despair. When he has rested complacently on his cultural creativity or on his technical progress, on his political institutions or on his religious systems, he has been thrown into disintegration and chaos; all the foundations of his personal, natural and cultural life have been shaken. As long as there has been human history, this is what has happened; in our period it has happened on a larger scale than ever before. Man's claim to be like God has been rejected once more; not one foundation of the life of our civilization has remained unshaken. As we read some of the passages from the prophets, we might easily imagine that we were reading the reports of eye-witnesses from Warsaw or Hiroshima or Berlin. Isaiah says: "Behold, the Lord maketh the earth empty and maketh it waste, and turneth it upside down and scattereth its inhabitants. . . . Towns fall to pieces; each man bolts his door; gladness has gone from the earth and pleasure is no more. The cities are left desolate; their gates are battered down; and few are left. . . . For earth has been polluted by the dwellers on its face . . . breaking the Eternal Covenant. Therefore, a curse is crushing the earth, and the guilty people must atone." Every one of these words describes the experience of the peoples of Europe and Asia. The most primitive and most essential foundations of life have been shaken. The destruction is such that we, who have not experienced it, cannot even imagine it. We have not experienced it; and we cannot believe that we could be caught in such a destruction. And yet, I see American soldiers walking through the ruins of these cities, thinking of their own country, and seeing with visionary clarity the doom of its towns and cities. I know that this has happened, and is still happening. There are soldiers who have become prophets, and their message is not very different from the message of the ancient Hebrew prophets. It is the message of the shaking of the foundations, and not those of their enemies, but rather those of their own country. For the prophetic spirit has not disappeared from the earth. Decades before the world wars, men judged the European civilization and prophesied its end in speech and print. There are among us people like these. They are like the refined instruments which register the shaking of the earth on far-removed sections of its surface. These people register the shaking of their civilization, its self-destructive trends, and its disintegration and fall, decades before the final catastrophe occurs. They have an invisible and almost infallible sensorium in their souls; and they have an irresistible urge to pronounce what they have registered, perhaps against their own wills. For no true prophet has ever prophesied voluntarily. It has been forced upon him by a Divine Voice to which he has not been able to close his ears. No man with a prophetic spirit likes to foresee and foresay the doom of his own period. It exposes him to a terrible anxiety within himself, to severe and often deadly attacks from others, and to the charge of pessimism and defeatism on the part of the majority of the people. Men desire to hear good tidings; and the masses listen to those who bring them. All the prophets of the Old and New Testaments, and others during the history of the Church, had the same experience. They all were contradicted by the false prophets, who announced salvation when there was no salvation. "The prophets prophesy falsely, and my people love to have it so", cries Jeremiah in despair. They called him a defeatist and accused him of being an enemy of his country. But is it a sign of patriotism or of confidence in one's people, its institutions and its way of life, to be silent when the foundations are shaking? Is the expression of optimism, whether or not it is justified, so much more valuable than the expression of truth, even if the truth is deep and dark? Most human beings, of course, are not able to stand the message of the shaking of the foundations. They reject and attack the prophetic minds, not because they really disagree with them, but because they sense the truth of their words and cannot receive it. They repress it in themselves; and they transform it into mockery or fury against those who *know* and dare to say that which they know. In which of these two groups do you consider yourselves to be? Among those who respond to the prophetic spirit, or among those who close their ears and hearts against it? I have always felt that there might be a few who are able to register the shaking of the foundations—who are able to stand this, and who are able, above all, to say what they know, because they are courageous enough to withstand the unavoidable enmity of the many. To those few my words are particularly directed.

Why were the prophets able to face what they knew, and then to pronounce it with such overwhelming power? Their power sprang from the fact that they did not really speak of the foundations of the earth as such, but of Him Who laid the foundations and would shake them; and that they did not speak of the doom of the nations as such, but of Him Who brings doom for the sake of His eternal justice and salvation. As the 102nd Psalm says: "Thy years are throughout all generations. Of old thou has laid the foundations of the earth, and the heavens are the work of thy hands. *They vanish,* but *thou shalt endure;* they wear out like a robe, thou changest them like garments. But thou art the same and thy years shall have no end. . . ." When the earth grows old and wears out, when nations and cultures die, the Eternal changes the garments of His infinite being. He is the foundation on which all foundations are laid; and this foundation cannot be shaken. There is something immovable, unchangeable, unshakeable, eternal, which becomes manifest in our passing and in the crumbling of our world. On the boundaries of the finite the infinite becomes visible; in the light of the Eternal the transitoriness of the temporal appears. The Greeks called

themselves "the mortals" because they experienced that
which is immortal. This is why the prophets were able
to face the shaking of the foundations. It is the only
way to look at the shaking without recoiling from it.
Or *is* it possible to be conscious of the approaching
doom, and yet to regard it with indifference and cynicism? Is it humanly possible to face the *end* cynically?
There are certainly some among us who are cynical
toward most of that which men create and praise. There
are some among us who are cynical about the present
situation of the world and the leaders of the world. We
may be cynical, of course, about the true motives behind all human action; we may be cynical about ourselves, our inner growth and our outer achievements.
We may be cynical about religion and about our
Churches, their doctrines, their symbols and their representatives. There is scarcely one thing about which
we may not be cynical. But we *can not* be cynical about
the shaking of the foundations of everything! I have
never encountered anyone who seriously was cynical
about that. I have seen much cynicism, particularly
among the younger people in Europe before the war.
But I know from abundant witnesses that this cynicism
vanished when the foundations of the world began to
shake at the beginning of the European catastrophe. We
can be cynical about the end only so long as we do not
have to see it, only so long as we feel safety in the place
in which our cynicism can be exercised. But if the foundations of this place and all places begin to crumble,
cynicism itself crumbles with them. And only two alter-
natives remain—despair, which is the certainty of eternal destruction, or faith, which is the certainty of eternal
salvation. "The world itself shall crumble, but . . . my
salvation knows no end." says the Lord. *This* is the al-

ternative for which the prophets stood. This is what we should call *religion,* or more precisely, the religious ground for all religion.

How could the prophets speak as they did? How could they paint these most terrible pictures of doom and destruction without cynicism or despair? It was because, beyond the sphere of destruction, they saw the sphere of salvation; because, in the doom of the temporal, they saw the manifestation of the Eternal. It was because they were certain that they belonged within the two spheres, the changeable *and* the unchangeable. For only he who is also beyond the changeable, not bound within it alone, can face the end. All others are compelled to escape, to turn away. How much of our lives consists in nothing but attempts to look away from the end! We often succeed in forgetting the end. But ultimately we fail; for we always carry the end with us in our bodies and our souls. And often whole nations and cultures succeed in forgetting the end. But ultimately they fail too, for in their lives and growth they always carry the end with them. Often the whole earth succeeds in making its creatures forget its end, but sometimes these creatures feel that their earth is beginning to grow old, and that its foundations are beginning to shake. For the earth always carries its end within it. We happen to live in a time when very few of us, very few nations, very few sections of the earth, will succeed in forgetting the end. For in these days the foundations of the earth *do* shake. May we *not* turn our eyes away; may we not close our ears and our mouths! But may we rather see, through the crumbling of a world, the rock of eternity and the salvation which has no end!

2

WE LIVE IN TWO ORDERS

Comfort ye, comfort ye, my people, saith your God.
Speak ye comfortably to Jerusalem, and cry unto her
That her warfare is accomplished,
That her iniquity is pardoned:
For she hath received of the Lord's hand
Double for all her sins.
The voice of him that crieth in the wilderness,
Prepare ye the way of the Lord,
Make straight in the desert a highway for our God.
Every valley shall be exalted,
And every mountain and hill shall be made low:
And the crooked shall be made straight,
And the rough places plain:
And the glory of the Lord shall be revealed,
And all flesh shall see it together:
For the mouth of the Lord has spoken it.
The voice said, Cry.
And he said, What shall I cry?
All flesh is grass,
And all the goodliness thereof is as the flower of the
  field:
The grass withereth, the flower fadeth:
Because the spirit of the Lord bloweth upon it:

Surely the people is grass.
The grass withereth, the flower fadeth:
But the word of our God shall stand forever.
O Zion, that bringest good tidings,
Get thee up into the high mountain;
O Jerusalem, that bringest good tidings,
Lift up thy voice with strength;
Lift it up, be not afraid;
Say unto the cities of Judah, Behold your God!
Behold, the Lord God will come with strong hand,
And his arm shall rule for him:
Behold, his reward is with him,
And his work before him.
He shall feed his flock like a shepherd:
He shall gather the lambs with his arm,
And carry them in his bosom,
And shall gently lead those that are with young.
Who hath measured the waters in the hollow of his
        hand,
And meted out heaven with the span,
And comprehended the dust of the earth in a
        measure,
And weighed the mountains in scales,
And the hills in a balance?
Who hath directed the Spirit of the Lord
Or being his counsellor hath taught him?
With whom took he counsel, and who instructed
        him,
And taught him in the path of judgment,

And taught him knowledge,
And shewed to him the way of understanding?
Behold, the nations are as a drop of a bucket,
And are counted as the small dust of the balance:
Behold, he taketh up the isles as a very little thing.
And Lebanon is not sufficient to burn,
Nor the beasts thereof sufficient for a burnt offering.
All nations before him are as nothing;
And they are counted to him less than nothing, and
    vanity.
To whom then will ye liken God?
Or what likeness will ye compare unto him?
The workman melteth a graven image,
And the goldsmith spreadeth it over with gold,
And casteth silver chains.
He that is so impoverished that he hath no oblation
Chooseth a tree that will not rot;
He seeketh unto him a cunning workman
To prepare a graven image, that shall not be moved.
Have ye not known? have ye not heard?
Hath it not been told you from the beginning?
Have ye not understood from the foundations of the
    earth?
It is he that sitteth upon the circle of the earth,
And the inhabitants thereof are as grasshoppers;
That stretcheth out the heavens as a curtain,
And spreadeth them out as a tent to dwell in:
That bringeth the princes to nothing;
He maketh the judges of the earth as vanity.

Yea, they shall not be planted;
Yea, they shall not be sown;
Yea, their stock shall not take root in the earth:
And he shall also blow upon them, and they shall
    wither,
And the whirlwind shall take them away as stubble.
To whom then will ye liken me,
Or shall I be equal? saith the Holy One.
Lift up your eyes on high,
And behold who hath created these things,
That bringeth out their host by number:
He calleth them all by names by the greatness of his
    might,
For that he is strong in power;
Not one faileth.
Why sayest thou, O Jacob,
And speakest, O Israel,
My way is hid from the Lord,
And my judgment is passed over from my God?
Hast thou not known? hast thou not heard?
That the everlasting God, the Lord,
The Creator of the ends of the earth,
Fainteth not, neither is weary?
There is no searching of his understanding.
He giveth power to the faint;
And to them that have no might he increaseth
    strength.
Even the youths shall faint and be weary.
And the young men shall utterly fall:

But they that wait upon the Lord shall renew their
     strength;
They shall mount up with wings as eagles;
They shall run and not be weary;
And they shall walk and not faint.

ISAIAH 40.

THESE TREMENDOUS WORDS WERE
written by that unknown prophet of the Babylonian
exile, whose sayings are united with those of the prophet
Isaiah and whom we therefore call the Second Isaiah.
Let us imagine that these words are being spoken to the
exiles of our time, to those in prisons and concentration
camps, separated from their husbands or wives, their
children or parents, to those toiling in despair in foreign
countries, to those in the hell of modern warfare. How
would they respond to such words, and how should we,
if they were spoken to us? Probably we should challenge,
ironically or angrily, their seeming pretentiousness; and
we should point to the immense gap between the ideal
situation, dramatized by the prophet, and the cata-
strophic reality in which we live. We should dismiss him
as an annoying optimist, not worthy of our attention.
Perhaps we should become bitter and full of hatred toward him. That would be our natural response to someone who desires to comfort us in a situation in which we
do not see any possible comfort and desperately dis-
believe any possible hope.

But the situation of the exiles in Babylon, sitting by
the rivers and weeping, was one of just such hopeless-
ness. The prophet must have expected this kind of reaction, for he spoke in a way that made the exiles listen

to him, 2500 years ago. And his words should be significant for us, the exiles of today. He was not less, but rather more, realistic than we are. He knew that such a situation was not a matter of chance and bad luck, but that it is the human situation, which no man and no period can escape. The human situation is one of finiteness—all flesh is grass and the grass withereth. It is one of sin—we receive double for all our sins. It is one of vanity and pride—we are brought to nothing and fall utterly. But in spite of his realistic knowledge of human nature and destiny the prophet gave comfort and consolation and hope to the exiled nation, to the exiles of all nations, to man who, as man, is exiled in this world.

The words of this great chapter sound like the rising and falling waves in a turbulent ocean. Darkness and light follow each other; after the depth of sin and punishment, the prophet announces forgiveness and liberation. But the wave falls, and the prophet asks himself how he could have made such an announcement, when all the goodness of mortal men is as the flower of the field, which fades because the breath of God blows upon it. But he does not remain in the depths of his melancholy: over against human mortality the word of God shall stand forever. There is something eternal to which we can cling: Be not afraid, the Lord God shall come with strong hand. So the wave rises, and then again it falls: the nations are as a drop of water and a piece of dust; all the nations are as nothing before Him, they are counted as less than nothing. . . . Again the wave rises: God stands above the circle of the earth, above all created things, above the highest and the lowest! And when once more the wave falls and the servant of God complains that he does not receive justice from God, the answer is that God acts beyond human expectation. He

gives power to the faint and to him that hath no might.
He increaseth strength. He acts paradoxically; He acts
beyond human understanding.

How shall we interpret these words? Is there a way
to unite the heights and depths contrasted in this chapter? Shall we understand the words of consolation and
hope as vain promises, never fulfilled in the past and
never to be fulfilled in any future? Shall we understand
them as an escape from the realization of man's real
situation, through mysticism and poetic elevation? If so,
what about the probing realism of the prophet's analysis
of the human situation? He saw history as it is, but at
the same time he looked beyond history to the ultimate
power and meaning and majesty of being. He knew two
orders of being: the human, political, historical order,
and the divine, eternal order. Because he knew these
two orders, he could speak as he did, moving continually
between the depth of human nothingness and the great
height of divine creativity.

Let us look at these orders, these different natures, and
their interrelation. In speaking of them we speak of ourselves, because we belong to both of them in every moment of our life and history.

The human order, the order of history, is primarily
the order of growing and dying. "Surely the people is
grass". Man's experience of melancholy, awakened by
fading and perishing nature, is symbolic of his transitoriness. Generations after generations grow up, struggle, suffer, enjoy and disappear. Should we take all this
seriously? Should we take it more seriously than the
growing and fading of the grass? The prophet, when
he was asked to speak to his nation, raised the question:
Why speak to them? They are grass. We could continue:
Why write and work and struggle for them? They are

grass. What matter, when after a few years all those for whom we wrote and spoke and struggled will have vanished? They were grass, the grass withered, the flowers faded. That is the order of history. *But* the other order appears at the horizon: the word of God shall stand forever.

Second, the order of history is an order of sin and punishment. The exile, following the destruction of Jerusalem, was, as all the prophets said, the punishment of the people for their sins. We do not like words such as "sin" and "punishment". They seem to us old-fashioned, barbaric, and invalid in the light of modern psychology. But whenever I have met exiles of high moral standards and insight, I have discovered that they feel responsible for what has happened within their own countries. And very often I have met citizens of democratic countries, citizens of this country, who have expressed a feeling of guilt for the situation of the world today. They were right, and the exiles were right: they are responsible, as are you and I. Whether or not we call it sin, whether or not we call it punishment, we are beaten by the consequences of our own failures. That is the order of history. But at the horizon the other order appears, saying that our struggles are not in vain, that our iniquity is pardoned.

There is a third element in the order of history, uniting finiteness and sin: the tragic law which controls the historical process, the law which ordains that human greatness utterly fall. There is human greatness in history. There are great and conquering nations and empires; there are even nations and empires which manifest a certain righteousness. There are princes and even good princes; there are judges and even just judges. There are states and constitutions and even states and

constitutions which provide a certain amount of freedom; there are social orders and even some which provide a certain amount of equality. There are creative
spirits and even some which have the power of knowledge and understanding. But just in being great and
powerful and righteous they touch the divine sphere,
and they become arrogant, and they are brought to nothing. They are without roots; they wither; the divine
storm blows over them, and they vanish. That is the
subject of Greek tragedy. That is the message of the
prophet to the nations of the world. They are all subject
to the law of tragic self-destruction—the bad and the
good, individuals and nations, the weak and the heroic.
And again the other order, the order beyond history and
tragedy, appears at the horizon: He gives power to the
faint and their strength is renewed, so that they shall
mount up with wings as eagles.

The order beyond the order of history is the divine
order. And it is paradoxical: men are like grass, but the
word of God spoken to them shall stand forever. Men
stand under the law of sin and punishment, but the
divine order breaks through it and brings forgiveness.
Men faint, falling from the height of their moral goodness and youthful power, and just when they have
fallen and are weakest, they run without weariness and
rise up with wings as eagles. God acts beyond all human
assumptions and valuations. He acts surprisingly, unex-
pectedly, paradoxically. The negative character of the
historical order is the positive character of the divine
order. The weak and despairing, the sinful and tragic
in the historical order are the strong and victorious in
the divine order.

A few chapters later, the prophet speaks of the paradoxical destiny of the servant, the elected nation. De-

scribed as a man of sorrows, acquainted with grief, it is
despised and rejected in the human order. Who does
not think, hearing these words, of the exiles not only of
Israel but of all nations of the world? But the divine
order appears. The exiled nation, or (as the Christians
later, historically wrong, spiritually right, interpreted it)
the Man on the Cross, represents another order, an order in which the weakest is the strongest, the most hu-
miliated, the most victorious. The historical, human
order is overcome by the suffering servant, the crucified
Saviour.

If we doubt this paradox, if we despair about our
human situation, if our exile is without hope or meaning
for us, the prophet should fill us with shame for the arrogance of our rationalism and the narrowness of our
moralism. He points to the creation of the world, of
mankind, of history. He asks, "Who has directed the
Spirit of God? With whom took He counsel and who
instructed Him and taught Him the path of justice?"
We always wish to teach God the path of justice. We
tell Him that He must punish the bad and reward the
good, especially in relation to ourselves. But He accepts
no counsel concerning the course of history, as He took
no counsel concerning the structure of the world, with
all its natural destruction, cruelty, and transitoriness.
The divine order cannot be judged according to the
measures of the historical order, the measures of human
comfort and morality, democracy and civilization. That
was the answer Job received from God when he struggled with Him about the unintelligible injustice of *his*
historical fate. God did not justify Himself in moral cat-
egories; He triumphantly pointed to the unexplorable
greatness of nature which cannot be measured according to the measure of human righteousness.

But if the divine order and the historical order have nothing to do with each other, how can the divine order concern us at all? How can eternity and forgiveness and divine help concern us if we are in the other order, the historical order, standing under the law of finiteness and weakness and punishment? How can the divine order comfort us in our misery? How can we listen to the words of the prophets which tell us of the end of our warfare? There are three answers to this question. First, the divine order is not the historical order; and we should not confuse these two orders. No life is able to overcome finiteness, sin, and tragedy. The illusions of our period have been that modern civilization *can* conquer them, and that we can achieve security in our own existence. Progress seemed to have conquered tragedy; the divine order seemed to be embodied in the progressive, historical order. But for nearly three decades our generation has received blow after blow, destroying that illusion, and driving to despair and cynicism those who wanted to transform, and thought they could transform, the historical order into a divine order. Let us learn from the catastrophe of our time at least the fact that *no* life and *no* period are able to overcome finiteness, sin, and tragedy.

The second answer is that there is another order to which we, as human beings, belong, an order which makes man *always* dissatisfied with what is given to him. Man transcends everything in the historical order, all the heights and depths of his own existence. He passes, as no other being is able to pass, beyond the limits of his given world. He participates in something infinite, in an order which is not transitory, not self-destructive, not tragic, but eternal, holy, and blessed. Therefore, when he listens to the prophetic word, when he hears of the everlasting God and of the greatness of His power and the mystery of His acts, a response is awakened in the depth of his soul; the infinite within him is touched. Every man knows, in some depth of his soul, that that is true. Our despair itself, our inability to escape ourselves in life and in death, witnesses to our infinity.

The third answer is that the two orders, the historical and the eternal, although they can never become the same, are within each other. The historical order is not separated from the eternal order. What is new in the prophets and in Christianity, beyond all paganism, old and new, is that the eternal order reveals itself in the historical order. The suffering servant of God and the enemies because of whom he suffers, the Man on the Cross and those who fainted under the Cross, the exiled and persecuted in all periods of history, have all transformed history. The strong in history fall; the strength of each of us is taken from us. But those who seem weak in history finally shape history, because they are bound to the eternal order. We are not a lost generation because we are a suffering, destroyed generation. Each of us belongs to the eternal order, and the prophet speaks to all of us: Comfort ye, comfort ye, my people!

3

THE PARADOX OF THE BEATITUDES

And he lifted up his eyes on his disciples, and said, Blessed be ye poor: for yours is the kingdom of God. Blessed are ye that hunger now: for ye shall be filled. Blessed are ye that weep now: for ye shall laugh. Blessed are ye, when men shall hate you, and when they shall separate you from their company, and shall reproach you, and cast out your name as evil, for the Son of Man's sake. Rejoice ye in that day, and leap for joy: for, behold, your reward is great in heaven: for in the like manner did their fathers unto the prophets. But woe unto you that are rich! for ye have received your consolation. Woe unto you that are full! for ye shall hunger. Woe unto you that laugh now! for ye shall mourn and weep. Woe unto you, when all men shall speak well of you! for so did their fathers to the false prophets.

LUKE 6:20-26.

READERS AND STUDENTS OF THE NEW Testament often find that it is not the refined argument of Paul or the mystical wisdom of John, but the simple sayings of Jesus, as recorded by the first three evangelists, which are the most difficult to interpret. The words

24

of Jesus seem so clear and straightforward and adequate that it is hard to imagine that anybody could miss the meaning. But when we are asked to express the meaning in our own words, we discover one level of meaning after another. We realize that words of Jesus which we have known since our earliest childhood are incomprehensible to us. And if we try to penetrate them, we are driven from one depth to another; we are never able to exhaust them. Nothing seems simpler, and yet nothing is more perplexing, than, for instance, the Lord's Prayer, the Parables, and the Beatitudes.

We have heard the four Beatitudes and the four Woes as Luke reports them. Their meaning seems unmistakable. The poor, those who are hungry *now,* those who weep *now,* those who are isolated and insulted, are praised, congratulated, so to speak, because they can expect precisely the opposite of their present situation. And the rich, those who are full, those who laugh, those who are popular and respected, are pitied, because they must expect precisely that which is contrary.

Two questions arise. *What* is promised and *to whom* is it promised? What is the kingdom which is to be owned by the poor, and who are the poor who shall own it? And who are the rich against whom the Woes shall be directed, and *what* shall happen to them?

Matthew tried to answer these questions. He said that the poor are the poor in spirit, and that those who hunger, hunger after righteousness. He said that those who weep, mourn for the state of the world. And to them is promised the kingdom of heaven, the vision of the Divine Spirit, the comfort and mercy of the realm of God.

Is Matthew's interpretation right? Or has Matthew, and have the official Christian Churches, following him, spiritualized the Beatitudes? Or, on the other hand, has Luke, and have the many sectarian and revolutionary movements, following him, distorted the Beatitudes from a materialistic point of view? Both assertions have been made and both are wrong. If we want the true answer, we must look at those to whom Jesus spoke. He spoke to two kinds of people. One kind lived with their hearts turned toward the *coming* stage of the world. They were poorly adjusted to things as they were. They were suffering under the conditions of their lives. Many were disinherited, insecure, hungry, oppressed. There is no distinction made in the Beatitudes between spiritual and material want, and there is no distinction made between spiritual and material fulfillment. Those to whom Jesus spoke were in need of both. Neither the prophets nor Jesus spiritualized the message of the Kingdom. Nor did they understand it and interpret it to say that the Kingdom would come as the result of a merely material revolution. Christianity pronounces the unity of body and soul. The Beatitudes praise those who will be fulfilled in their whole being. But the other kind of people to whom Jesus spoke were those to whom He promised the Woes. They were unbroken in their relation to the present stage of the world. They lived with their hearts in things as they are. They were well-established in their lives; they enjoyed prestige, power and security. Jesus threatened them spiritually *and* materially. They were bound to *this* eon, and they were to vanish with *this* eon. They had no treasure beyond it.

The situation of the people of Galilee to whom Jesus spoke is still our situation. The Woes are promised today to all of us who are well off, respected, and secure, not simply because we *have* such security and respect, but because it inevitably binds us, with an almost irresistible power, to this eon, to things as they are. And the Beatitudes are promised today to all of us who are without security and popularity, who are mourning in body and soul. And they are promised not simply because we lack so much, but because the very fact of our lacks and our sorrows may turn our hearts away from things as they are, toward the coming eon. The Beatitudes do not glorify those who are poor and in misery, individuals or classes, *because* they are poor. The Woes are not promised to those who are rich and secure, classes or individuals, *because* they are rich. If this were so, Jesus could not have promised to the poor the reversal of their situation. He praises the poor in so far as they live in *two* worlds, the present world and the world to come. And He threatens the rich in so far as they live in one world alone.

This brings a tremendous tension into our lives. We live in two orders, one of which is a reversal of the other. The *coming* order is always coming, shaking *this* order, fighting with it, conquering it and conquered by it. The coming order is always at hand. But one can never say: "It is here! It is there!" One can never grasp it. But one can be grasped by it. And whenever one is grasped by it, he is rich, even if he be poor in this order. His wealth is his participation in the coming order, in its battles, its victories and defeats. He is blessed, he may rejoice and leap even when he is isolated and insulted, because his isolation belongs to this order, while he belongs to the other order! He is blessed, while they who cast out his name are to be pitied. By their dread and despair, and by their hatred of him, they prove that the Woes Jesus has directed against them have already become real. They lose the one and only order they have; they disintegrate in body and spirit. Perhaps we are right to consider the catastrophe of our present world as a fulfillment of the Woes which Jesus directed against a rich, abundant, laughing, self-congratulating social order. But if we believe this, we can also believe that those who have become poor and hungry and sorrowing and persecuted in this catastrophe are those in whom the other order is made manifest. They may betray it, but they are called first. Only through the paradox of the Beatitudes can we begin to understand our own life and the life of our world.

4

THE TWO SERVANTS OF JAHWEH

Now, the Eternal cries, bring your case forward, ...
Now, Jacob's King cries, state your proofs.
Let us hear what happened in the past, that we may
  ponder it,
Or show me what is yet to be, that we may watch
  the outcome.
Yes, let us hear what is to come, that we may be
  sure that you are gods;
Come, do something or other that we may marvel at
  the sight!
Why, you are things of naught; you can do nothing
  at all!
Here is one I have raised from the north;
I have called him by name from the east.
He shall trample down rulers as morter, like a potter
  treading clay.
Now, we predicted this beforehand.
Who foretold it, that we might hail it true?
No one predicted it, no one announced it,
Not a word ever fell from your mouths. . . .
As for your idols, I see no one, not a prophet in their
  midst
To answer my inquiries.

*They are all an empty nothing; all they do is utterly
    inane.*
Their metal images are all futile, all vain.

ISAIAH 41:21-26, 28-29.

A DRAMATIC SCENE IS DESCRIBED IN
the words of the prophet. Jahweh, as judge and party
at the same time, calls the gods of the nations to a heavenly disputation, to be witnessed by the peoples of the
world. They are to discuss which god has proved to be
the true God. The true God must be He Who is the
Lord of history. The final decision is that Jahweh is the
God of history, and therefore the god who is really God.
Jahweh is the God of history, because He has shown
through His prophets that He understands the meaning
of history, and that He knows the past and the future,
the beginning and end, of all things. In showing that,
He proves that He *makes* history, and that it is He Who
has raised Cyrus, the destroyer of the power of the Jewish nation and the liberator of its remnants. The gods
of the nations cannot answer. For they did not know of
that act; they did not predict it; and they did not perform it. The disputation ends with the pronouncement
that these gods are all vain, that their works are as nothing, and that their images are as mere wind and illusion.
It is Jahweh alone Who is God, for He is the God of
history.

Seldom in history have men been as disturbed about
history as we are today. We desire urgently to catch at
least a glimpse of the future, of wisdom and prophecy.
It is not just a few thousand Jewish exiles, to whom
our prophet speaks by the rivers of Babylon, but ten

million exiles from all over the world, who try passionately to penetrate the darkness of their future. And with them, a great many other men long for a strong, inspiring word concerning the future of mankind.

But those who have the power to shape the future fundamentally contradict each other. Political leaders declare solemnly that it is almost impossible to carry the burden of their office at this time. Ministers at home and in the army can only describe in negative terms the object of their people's death and sacrifice. Those who have to speak to the people of the enemy soon realize that they can say nothing of real promise on the political plane. Only the prophets of disaster-without-hope give evidence of complete certainty. But they are not the prophets of God.

We should not expect the darkness of our history to be dispersed soon, either by new conferences or by clever political strategy. Our darkness, uncertainty, and helplessness in regard to the future have depths that are more profound. We do not receive an answer concerning the future, because we ask questions of those who cannot know the future, the gods who are as vanity, the gods of the nations, who are as nothing beside the God of history. Every man tries to wrest an oracle from the god of *his* nation through the mouths of his priests, the mighty and wise. And every man succeeds. All men throughout the world are flooded with oracles from the gods of their nations and the gods of other nations. All men compare their oracles with others, and attempt to determine the most credible ones. But the darkness simply increases. All men speak of the future in terms of their own nations. Yet even the greatest nation is as nothing to the God of history. For no nation or alliance of nations can say that *it* is the meaning, the pur-

pose of history, that *it* is the nation or alliance which
holds the knowledge of the past and the power to shape
the future. The entire assembly of national gods must
fall finally under the Judgment of Jahweh, which condemns it as a thing of naught, as a thing incapable of
doing anything at all. We receive so many oracles, but
no prophecies, only because we refuse to turn to the
source of prophecy, the God of history.

Jahweh revealed Himself through Israel's pain as
the God Who is the first and the last, the beginning and
the end, of history. A complete national breakdown
alone made the remnants of Israel ready to receive this
revelation in its universal significance. But whenever the
Jewish nation used that revelation as an excuse for national pride, and transformed Jahweh into a merely
national god, another breakdown followed. For Jahweh
as a national god is always condemned by Jahweh the
God of history. The mystery of Judaism today lies in
that fact.

Our prophet describes two very great figures: Cyrus,
the founder of the Persian Empire, the world-figure of
his time, called by the prophet the shepherd and the
anointed, the man of God's counsel; and the servant
of Jahweh who represents the saving power of innocent
suffering and death. The glorious founder of the Empire
had to be the servant of the servant of Jahweh. He had
to liberate the remnants of Israel, out of which the suffering servant arose.

I feel that the only solution of the historical problem
today lies in that prophetic concept. For there are two
forces in our battered world. One is the force of those
who, like the suffering servant of God, exist, unseen, in
all countries. We do not know where these servants
live, or what they will make of the future. But we know

that they exist, and that their suffering is not vain. They
are the hidden tools of the God of history. They are the
aged and the children, the young men and the young
women, the persecuted and the imprisoned, and all
those sacrificed for the sake of the future, for one small
stone in the building of the Kingdom of God, the cor-
nerstone of which is the perfect Servant of God. And
the second force of the world is the force of those who,
like Cyrus, rule Empires, and incorporate all the shame
and greatness of Empires. They are the men of God's
counsel, because they carry through His purposes in
the service of the suffering servants of Jahweh. But they
are not aware that they are instruments, as Cyrus was
not aware that he was God's man of counsel. They do
not know what shall become of their deeds. And if we
look to them in our attempts to grasp the future, we
shall not know either; if we look to them, we shall always
remain in darkness. But if we turn to the true servants
and to the true God whom they serve, the God of history, we shall know of the future. We can find the solution of the riddle of history as a whole, and of our particular history, in the figure of Cyrus in the service of
the servant of Jahweh.

5

MEDITATION: THE MYSTERY OF TIME

LET US MEDITATE ON THE MYSTERY OF time. Augustine points to the depth of this mystery, when he says, "If nobody asks me about it, I *know*. If I want to explain it to somebody who asks me about it, I do not know." There is something unspeakable about time, but this has not prevented the most profound religious minds from thinking and speaking about it. It is not vain speculation when the writer of the first part of the 90th Psalm confronts the eternity of God with the transitoriness of human existence. The melancholy experience of human finiteness drives him to utter the tremendous words of the psalm. It is not empty curiosity when Augustine tries, in his most personal book, the *Confessions,* to penetrate the ground of our temporality. We are not making an abstract statement, but are rather expressing a profound religious feeling, when we sing, "Time like an ever-rolling stream bears all its sons away". It is not mere philosophy, but a tragic feeling of life, which impels the earliest Greek philosophers to say that all things must return to their origin, suffering punishment, "according to the order of time". It is not merely in the interest of systematic theory that the Fourth Gospel uses again and again the phrase "eternal life" as the expression of the highest good, which is ever present in Christ. It was a religious event when Meister Eckhardt pointed to the "eternal now" within the flux of time, and when Soren Kierkegaard

34

pointed to the infinite significance of every moment as the "now" of decision.

Time is as inexhaustible as the ground of life itself. Even the greatest minds have each discovered only one aspect of it. But everyone, even the most simple mind, apprehends the meaning of time—namely, his own temporality. He may not be able to express his knowledge about time, but he is never separated from its mystery. His life, and the life of each of us, is permeated in every moment, in every experience, and in every expression, by the mystery of time. Time is our destiny. Time is our hope. Time is our despair. And time is the mirror in which we see eternity. Let me point to three of the many mysteries of time: its power to devour everything within its sphere; its power to receive eternity within itself; and its power to drive toward an ultimate end, a new creation.

Mankind has always realized that there is something fearful about the flux of time, a riddle which we cannot solve, and the solution of which we could not stand. We come from a past which is no more; we go into a future which is not yet; *ours* is the present. The past is ours only in so far as we have it still present; and the future is ours only in so far as we have it already present. We possess the past by memory, and the future by anticipation. But what is the nature of the present itself? If we look at it closely, we must say: it is a point without extension, the point in which the future becomes the past; when we say to ourselves, "This is the present," the moment has already been swallowed by the past. The present disappears the very instant we try to grasp it. The present cannot be caught; it is always gone. So it seems that we have nothing real—neither the past nor the future, nor even the present. Therefore, there is a dreaming character about our existence, which the psalmist indicates, and which religious visionaries have described in so many ways.

Time, however, could not even give us a place on which to stand, if it were not characterized by that second mystery, its power to receive eternity. There is no present in the mere stream of time; but the present is real, as our experience witnesses. And it is real because eternity breaks into time and gives it a real present. We could not even say "now," if eternity did not elevate *that* moment above the ever-passing time. Eternity is always present; and its presence is the cause of our having the present at all. When the psalmist looks at God, for Whom a thousand years are like one day, he is looking at that eternity which alone gives him a place on which he can stand, a "now" which has infinite reality and infinite significance. In every moment that we say "now", something temporal and something eternal are united. Whenever a human being says, "Now I am living; now I am really present", resisting the stream which drives the future into the past, eternity *is*. In each such "now", eternity is made manifest; in every real "now", eternity is present. Let us think for a moment of the way in which we are living our lives in our period of history. Have we not lost a real present by always being driven forward, by our constant running, in our indefatigable activism, toward the future? We suppose the future to be better than any present; but there is always another future beyond the next future, again and again without a present, that is to say, without eternity. According to the Fourth Gospel eternal life is a *present* gift: he, who listens to Christ, has eternity already. He is no longer subject to the driving of time. In him the "now" becomes a "now eternal". We have lost the real "now", the "now eternal"; we have, I am afraid, lost eternal life in so far as it creates the real present.

There is another element in time, its third mystery, which makes us look at the future; for time does not return, nor repeat itself: it runs forward; it is always unique; it ever creates the new. There is within it a drive toward an end, unknown, never to be reached in time itself, always intended and ever fleeing. Time runs toward the "future eternal". This is the greatest of all the mysteries of time. It is the mystery of which the prophets, Christ, and the Apostles have spoken. The eternal is the solution of the riddle of time. Time does not drive toward an endless self-repetition, nor to an empty return to its beginning. Time is not meaningless. It has a hidden meaning—salvation. It has a hidden goal—the Kingdom of God. It brings about a hidden reality—the new creation. The infinite significance of every moment of time is this: in it we decide, and are decided about, with respect to our eternal future.

6

THE ESCAPE FROM GOD

O Lord, thou hast searched me and known me.
Thou knowest my downsitting and mine uprising,
Thou understandest my thought afar off.
Thou compassest my path and my lying down,
And art acquainted with all my ways.
For there is not a word in my tongue,
But, lo, O Lord, thou knowest it altogether.
Thou hast beset me behind and before,
And laid thine hand upon me.
Such knowledge is too wonderful for me;
It is high, I cannot attain unto it.
Whither shall I go from thy spirit?
Or whither shall I flee from thy presence?
If I ascend up into heaven, thou art there;
If I make my bed in hell, behold, thou art there.
If I take the wings of the morning,
And dwell in the uttermost parts of the sea,
Even there shall thy hand lead me,
And thy right hand shall hold me.
If I say, Surely the darkness shall cover me,
Even the night shall be light about me.
Yea, the darkness hideth not from thee,
But the night shineth as the day.

The darkness and the light are both alike to thee.

For thou hast possessed my reins;

Thou hast covered me in my mother's womb.

I will praise thee, for I am fearfully and wonderfully made;

Marvellous are thy works; and that my soul knoweth right well.

My substance was not hid from thee, when I was made in secret,

And curiously wrought in the lowest parts of the earth.

Thine eyes did see my substance, yet being unperfect;

And in thy book all my members were written, which in continuance

Were fashioned, when as yet there was none of them.

How precious also are thy thoughts unto me, O God!

How great is the sum of them!

If I should count them, they are more in number than the sand.

When I awake, I am still with thee.

Surely thou wilt slay the wicked, O God:

Depart from me, therefore, ye bloody men.

For they speak against thee wickedly,

And thine enemies take thy name in vain.

Do not I hate them, O Lord, that hate thee?

And am not I grieved with those that rise up against thee?

I hate them with perfect hatred.

I count them mine enemies.
Search me, O God, and know my heart;
Try me and know my thoughts;
And see if there be any wicked way in me,
And lead me in the way everlasting.

PSALM 139.

"WHERE COULD I GO FROM THY SPIRIT, and where could I flee from Thy Face?" These are the central words of the great 139th Psalm. They state in the form of a question *the inescapable Presence of God.* Let us consider this statement, and the powerful images in which the psalmist tries to express it. God is inescapable. He is God only *because* He is inescapable. And only that which *is* inescapable is God.

There is no place to which we could flee from God which is outside of God. "If I ascend to the heavens, Thou art there." It seems very natural for God to be in heaven, and very unnatural for us to wish to ascend to heaven in order to escape Him. But that is just what the idealists of all ages have tried to do. They have tried to leap towards the heaven of perfection and truth, of justice and peace, where God is not wanted. That heaven is a heaven of man's making, without the driving restlessness of the Divine Spirit and without the judging presence of the Divine Face. But such a place is a "no place"; it is a "utopia", an idealistic illusion. "If I make hell my home, behold, Thou art there." Hell or Sheol, the habitation of the dead, would seem to be the right place to hide from God. And that is where all those who long for death, in order to escape the Divine Demands, attempt to flee. I am convinced

that there is not one amongst us who has not at some
time desired to be liberated from the burden of his existence by stepping out of it. And I know that there are
some amongst us for whom this longing is a daily temptation. But everyone knows in the depth of his heart
that death would not provide an escape from the inner
demand made upon him. "If I take the wings of the dawn
and dwell in the midst of the sea, Thy Hand would even
fall on me there, and Thy right Hand would grasp me."
To fly to the ends of the earth would not be to escape
from God. Our technical civilization attempts just that,
in order to be liberated from the knowledge that it lacks
a centre of life and meaning. The modern way to flee
from God is to rush ahead and ahead, as quickly as the
beams before sunrise, to conquer more and more space
in every direction, in every humanly possible way, to
be always active, to be always planning, and to be always preparing. But God's Hand falls upon us; and it
has fallen heavily and destructively upon our fleeing
civilization; our flight proved to be vain. "When I think
that the darkness shall cover me, that night shall hide
me, I know at the same time that the darkness is not
dark to Thee, and that night is as bright as day." To
flee into darkness in order to forget God is not to escape
Him. For a time we may be able to hurl Him out of our
consciousness, to reject Him, to refute Him, to argue
convincingly for His non-existence, and to live very comfortably without Him. But ultimately we know that it
is not He Whom we reject and forget, but that it is rather
some distorted picture of Him. And we know that we
can argue against Him, only because He impels us to
attack Him. There is no escape from God through
forgetfulness.

"Where could I go from Thy Spirit? O, where could

I flee from Thy Face?" The poet who wrote those words
to describe the futile attempt of man to escape God certainly believed that man *desires* to escape God. He is not
alone in his conviction. Men of all kinds, prophets and
reformers, saints and atheists, believers and unbelievers,
have the same experience. It is safe to say that a man
who has never tried to flee God has never experienced
the God Who is really God. When I speak of God, I do
not refer to the many gods of our own making, the gods
with whom we can live rather comfortably. For there
is no reason to flee a god who is the perfect picture of
everything that is good in man. Why try to escape from
such a far-removed ideal? And there is no reason to flee
from a god who is simply the universe, or the laws of
nature, or the course of history. Why try to escape from
a reality of which we are a part? There is no reason to
flee from a god who is nothing more than a benevolent
father, a father who guarantees our immortality and
final happiness. Why try to escape from someone who
serves us so well? No, those are not pictures of God, but
rather of man, trying to make God in his own image
and for his own comfort. They are the products of man's
imagination and wishful thinking, justly denied by every
honest atheist. A god whom we can easily bear, a god
from whom we do not have to hide, a god whom we do
not hate in moments, a god whose destruction we never
desire, is not God at all, and has no reality.

Friedrich Nietzsche, the famous atheist and ardent
enemy of religion and Christianity, knew more about
the power of the idea of God than many faithful Christians. In a symbolic story, when Zarathustra, the prophet
of a higher humanity, says to the Ugliest Man, the murderer of God, "You could not bear him to see you, always to see you through and through. . . . You took re-

venge on the witness. . . . You are the murderer of
God", the Ugliest Man agrees with Zarathustra and re-
plies, "He *had* to die." For God, according to the Ugliest
Man, looks with eyes that see everything; He peers into
man's ground and depth, into his hidden shame and
ugliness. The God Who sees everything, and man also,
is the God Who has to die. Man cannot stand that
such a Witness live.

Are *we* able to stand such a Witness? The psalmist
says, "O Lord, thou hast searched me and known me."
Who can stand to be known so thoroughly even in the
darkest corners of his soul? Who does not want to escape
such a Witness? And who does not want to become one
who can deny God in theory and practice, an atheist?
"Thou knowest when I sit down, and when I stand up.
. . . Walking or resting, I am judged by Thee; and all
my ways are open to Thee." God knows what we *are;*
and He knows what we *do.* Who does not hate a companion who is always present on every road and in every
place of rest? Who does not want to break through the
prison of such a perpetual companionship? "Thou dis-
cernest my thoughts from afar . . . Lord, there is not a
word on my tongue which Thou knowest not." The
Divine Presence is spiritual. It penetrates the innermost
parts of our own spirits. Our entire inner life, our
thoughts and desires, our feelings and imaginations, are
known to God. The final way of escape, the most intimate of all places, is held by God. That fact is the hardest of all to accept. The human resistance against such
relentless observation can scarcely be broken. Every
psychiatrist and confessor is familiar with the tremendous force of resistance in each personality against even
trifling self-revelations. Nobody wants to be *known,* even
when he realizes that his health and salvation depend

upon such a knowledge. We do not even wish to be known by ourselves. We try to hide the depths of our souls from our own eyes. We refuse to be our own witness. How then can we stand the mirror in which nothing can be hidden?

Is the Ugliest Man right? The Ugliest Man is a symbol of the ugliness in each one of us, and the symbol of our will to hide at least something from God and from ourselves. The Ugliest Man seems to be right, when we consider the support he receives from saints, theologians, and reformers. Martin Luther was as strongly grasped as the psalmist by the penetrating Presence of God. He stated that in every creature God is deeper, more internal, and more present than the creature is to himself, and that God embraces all things, is within all things. But this most intimate Presence of God created the same feeling in Luther that it did in Nietzsche. He desired that God not be God. "I did not love God. I hated the just God . . . and was indignant towards Him, if not in wicked revolt, at least in silent blasphemy." Following St. Bernard, the great master of religious self-observation, he continued, "We cannot love God, and therefore we cannot will Him to exist. We cannot want Him to be most wise . . . and most powerful." Luther was terribly shocked when he recognized this hatred for God within himself. He was not able to escape as shrewdly as his theological masters, who recommended that he not think constantly of the searching Presence of God, and thus avoid the blasphemy of hating God. Luther knew with the psalmist that no escape is possible. "Thou art behind and before me, and on every side of me, laying Thy Hand upon me." God stands on each side of us, before and behind us. There is no way out.

The pious man of the Old Testament, the mystical saint of the Middle Ages, the reformer of the Christian Church, and the prophet of atheism are all united through that tremendous human experience: man cannot stand the God Who is really God. Man tries to escape God, and hates Him, because he cannot escape Him. The protest against God, the will that there be no God, and the flight to atheism are all genuine elements of profound religion. And only on the basis of these elements has religion meaning and power.

Christian theology and religious instruction speak of the Divine Omnipresence, which is the doctrine that God is everywhere, and of the Divine Omniscience, which is the doctrine that God knows everything. It is difficult to avoid such concepts in religious thought and education. But they are at least as dangerous as they are useful. They make us picture God as a thing with superhuman qualities, omnipresent like an electric power field, and omniscient like a superhuman brain. Such concepts as "Divine Omnipresence" and "Divine Omniscience" transform an overwhelming religious experience into an abstract, philosophical statement, which can be accepted and rejected, defined, redefined, and replaced. In making God an object besides other objects, the existence and nature of which are matters of argument, theology supports the escape to atheism. It encourages those who are interested in denying the threatening Witness of their existence. The first step to atheism is always a theology which drags God down to the level of doubtful things. The game of the atheist is then very easy. For he is perfectly justified in destroying such a phantom and all its ghostly qualities. And because the theoretical atheist is just in his destruction, the practical atheists (all of us) are willing to use his argument to support our own attempt to flee God.

Let us therefore forget these concepts, *as* concepts, and try to find their genuine meaning within our own experience. We all know that we cannot separate ourselves at any time from the world to which we belong. There is no ultimate privacy or final isolation. We are always held and comprehended by something that is greater than we are, that has a claim upon us, and that demands response from us. The most intimate motions within the depths of our souls are not completely our own. For they belong also to our friends, to mankind, to the universe, and to the Ground of all being, the aim of our life. Nothing can be hidden ultimately. It is always reflected in the mirror in which nothing can be concealed. Does anybody really believe that his most secret thoughts and desires are not manifest in the whole of being, or that the events within the darkness of his subconscious or in the isolation of his consciousness do not produce eternal repercussions? Does anybody really believe that he can escape from the responsibility for what he has done and thought in secret? Omniscience means that our mystery is manifest. Omnipresence means that our privacy is public. The centre of our whole being is involved in the centre of all being; and the centre of all being rests in the centre of our being. I do not believe that any serious man can deny that experience, no matter how he may express it. And if he has had the experience, he has also met something within him that makes him desire to escape the consequences of it. For man is not equal to his own experience; he attempts to forget it; and he knows that he *cannot* forget it.

Is there a release from that tension? Is it possible to

overcome the hatred for God and the will that there
be no God, that there be no man? Is there a way to triumph over our shame before the perpetual Witness
and over the despair which is the burden of our inescapable responsibility? Nietzsche offers a solution which
shows the utter impossibility of atheism. The Ugliest
Man, the murderer of God, subjects himself to Zarathustra, because Zarathustra has recognized him, and
looked into his depth with divine understanding. The
murderer of God finds God in man. He has not suc-
ceeded in killing God at all. God has returned in Zarathustra, and in the new period of history which Zarathustra announces. God is always revived in something or
somebody; He cannot be murdered. The story of every
atheism is the same.

The psalmist offers another solution. "I praise Thee
for the awful wonder of my birth; Thy work is wonderful. For Thou didst form my being, and weave me together in my mother's womb. None of my bones were
hidden from Thee, when I was made in secret and
molded in the lowest parts of the earth." Using the old
mythological idea that men are formed in the abyss
below the earth, he points to the mystery of creation,
not to the creation in general, but to the creation of his
own being. The God Whom he cannot flee is the Ground
of his being. And this being, his nature, soul, and body,
is a work of infinite wisdom, awful and wonderful. The
admiration of the Divine Wisdom overcomes the horror
of the Divine Presence in this passage. It points to the
friendly presence of an infinitely creative wisdom. It is
this mood which runs generally throughout the Old
Testament. A great scholar, with whom I conversed
once on the will to death in every life, exhibited the same
mood, when he said, "Let us not forget that life is also

friendly." There is a grace in life. Otherwise we could
not live. The eyes of the Witness we cannot stand are
also the eyes of One of infinite wisdom and supporting
benevolence. The centre of being, in which our own
centre is involved, is the source of the gracious beauty
which we encounter again and again in the stars and
mountains, in flowers and animals, in children and mature personalities.

But there is something more to the psalmist's solution.
He does not simply consider the creative Ground of his
being. He also looks to the creative destiny of his life.
"Thine eyes saw the sum total of my days, and in Thy
book they were all written. They were counted before
they ever came into existence." The psalmist uses another old mythical symbol, which is the record of earthly
events in an heavenly book. He expresses poetically
what we today call the belief in an ultimate meaning of
our life. Our days are written and counted; they are
not merely accidental. He Who sees us most intimately
looks at the vision of our whole life. We belong to this
whole; we have a place of the utmost importance within
it. As individuals and as a group, we have an ultimate
destiny. And whenever we sense this ultimate destiny,
whether or not it appears as great or insignificant, we
are aware of God, the Ground and centre of all meaning.
We can join in the psalmist's cry of admiration: "How
mysterious Thy thoughts are to me, O God! How great
the sum of them is! If I were to count them, they would
outnumber the sands; and if I were to come to the end
of them, the span of my life would be like Thine!" The
psalmist thus conquers the horror of the all-reflecting
mirror and of the never-sleeping Witness by his recog-
nition of the infinite mystery of life, its Ground and
its meaning.

But suddenly, at the climax of his meditation, the psalmist turns away from God. He remembers that there is a dark element in the picture of his life—enmity against God, wickedness, and bloody deeds. And since this element disturbs his picture, he asks God to eradi- cate it. In sudden rage, he shouts, "If Thou wouldst but slay the wicked, O God, and make the men of blood depart from me, who oppose Thee in their thoughts, and utter Thy name in their crimes! Should I not hate them that hate Thee, O Lord? Should I not despise them? I hate them with the deadliest hatred. They are also my enemies!" These words should disturb anyone who thinks that the problem of life can be solved by meditation and religious elevation. Their mood is quite different from that of the previous words. Praise turns into curse. And the trembling of the heart before the all-observing God is replaced by wrath towards men. This wrath makes the psalmist feel that he is equal with God, the God from Whom he wished to flee into dark- ness and death. God must hate those whom he hates; and God's enemies must be *his* enemies. He has just spoken of the infinite distance between his thoughts and God's thoughts; but he has forgotten. Religious fanati- cism appears, that fanaticism which has inflamed the ar- rogance of Churches, the cruelty of the moralists, and the inflexibility of the orthodox. The sin of religion appears in one of the greatest Psalms. It is that sin which has dis- torted the history of the Church and the vision of Chris- tianity, and which was not fully avoided even by Paul and John. Of course, we whose religious experience is poor and whose feeling of God is weak should not judge too harshly those whose lives burned with the fire of the Divine Presence and spread this fire ardently all over the world. Nevertheless, the sin of religion is real; and it contradicts the Spirit of Him, Who forbade His disciples again and again to hate His enemies as the enemies of God.

Yet, a change of thought and feeling brings the psalmist suddenly back to the beginning of his poem. He feels quite obviously that something may have been wrong in what he has uttered. He does not know what is wrong; but he is certain that God knows. And so he concludes with one of the greatest prayers of all time: "Search me, O God, and know my heart. Try me and know my thoughts. And see if there be any false way in me; and lead me the perfect way." At this moment he *asks* God to do what, according to the first words of the Psalm, he does relentlessly anyway. The psalmist has overcome his wavering between the will to flee God and the will to be equal with God. He has found that the final solution lies in the fact that the Presence of the Witness, the Presence of the centre of all life within the centre of *his* life, implies both a radical attack on his existence, and the ultimate meaning of his existence. We are known in a depth of darkness through which we ourselves do not even dare to look. And at the same time, we are seen in a height of a fullness which surpasses our highest vision. That infinite tension is the atmosphere in which religion lives. In that tension Luther conquered his hatred for God, when he discovered in Christ the Crucified the perfect symbol for our human situation. It is the tension in which modern man lives, even though he may have lost the way to traditional religion. A human being can be ultimately judged by whether or not he has reached and can stand that tension. To endure it is more horrible and more difficult than anything else in the world. And yet, to endure it is the only way by which we can attain to the ultimate meaning, joy, and freedom in our lives. Each of us is called to endure. May each of us have the strength and the courage to bear that vocation! For it is to that vocation that we are called as men.

7

THE DEPTH OF EXISTENCE

*But God hath revealed them unto us by his Spirit.
for the Spirit searcheth all things, yea, the deep
things of God.*   I CORINTHIANS 2:10.

Out of the depths have I cried unto thee, O Lord.
                                              PSALM 130:1.

FROM THE WORDS OF PAUL'S LETTER TO
the Corinthians, let us concentrate on one verse: "The
Spirit searcheth all things, yea, the deep things of God."
And from this verse, let us make one word—the word
"deep"—the subject of our meditation.

And from the 130th Psalm let us concentrate on that
one verse: "Out of the depths I have cried unto Thee,
O Lord"; and let us make one word—the word "depth"
—also the subject of our meditation.

The words "deep" and "depth" are used in our daily
life, in poetry and philosophy, in the Bible, and in
many other religious documents, to indicate a spiritual
attitude, although the words themselves are taken from
a spatial experience. Depth is a dimension of space; yet
at the same time it is a symbol for a spiritual quality.
Most of our religious symbols have this character, re-
minding us of our finitude and our bondage to things
that are visible. We are and we remain sensuous beings

52

even when we deal with spiritual things. There is, on the other hand, a great wisdom in our language. It is the embodiment of innumerable experiences of the past. It is not by chance alone that we use certain visible symbols and do not use others. Therefore, it is often useful to find the reasons for the choices of the collective mind of former generations. It may become of ultimate significance to us, when we see what is implied in the use of terms like "deep", "depth", and "profound", for the expression of our spiritual life. It may give us the impulse to strive for our own depth.

"Deep" in its spiritual use has two meanings: it means either the opposite of "shallow", or the opposite of "high". Truth is deep and not shallow; suffering is depth and not height. Both the light of truth and the darkness of suffering are deep. There is a depth in God, and there is a depth out of which the psalmist cries to God. Why is truth deep? And why is suffering deep? And why is the same spatial symbol used for both experiences? These questions shall guide our meditation.

All visible things have a surface. Surface is that side of things which first appears to us. If we look at it, we know what things *seem* to be. Yet if we act according to what things and persons *seem* to be, we are disappointed. Our expectations are frustrated. And so we try to penetrate below the surfaces in order to learn what things really are. Why have men always asked for truth? Is it because they have been disappointed with the surfaces, and have known that the truth which does *not* disappoint dwells below the surfaces in the depth? And therefore, men have dug through one level after another. What seemed true one day was experienced as superficial the next. When we encounter a person, we receive an impression. But often if we act accordingly we are disappointed by his actual behavior. We pierce a deeper level of his character, and for some time experience less disappointment. But soon he may do something which is contrary to all our expectations; and we realize that what we know about him is still superficial. Again we dig more deeply into his true being.

Science has been carried on in this way. Science questions the common assumptions which seem to be true to everyone, to the layman as well as to the average scholar. Then the genius comes and asks for the basis of these accepted assumptions; when they are proved not to be true, an earthquake in science occurs out of the depth. Such earthquakes occurred when Copernicus asked if our sense-impressions could be the ground of astronomy, and when Einstein questioned whether there is an absolute point from which the observer could look at the motions of things. An earthquake occurred when Marx questioned the existence of an intellectual and moral history independent of its economic and social basis. It occurred in the most eruptive way when the first philosophers questioned what everybody had taken for granted from times immemorial—being itself. When they became conscious of the astonishing fact, underlying all facts, that there is something and not nothing, an unsurpassable depth of thought was reached.

In the light of these great and daring steps toward the deep things of our world, we should look at ourselves and at the opinions we take for granted. And we should see what there is in these things of prejudice, derived from our individual preferences and social surroundings. We should be shocked to notice how little of our spiritual world is deeper than the surface, how little would be able to withstand a serious blow. Some-

thing terribly tragic happens in all periods of man's spiritual life: truths, once deep and powerful, discovered by
the greatest geniuses through profound suffering and
incredible labor, become shallow and superficial when
used in daily discussion. How can and how does this
tragedy occur? It can and does unavoidably occur, because there can be no depth without the way to the
depth. Truth without the way to truth is dead; if it still
be used, it contributes only to the surface of things.
Look at the student who knows the content of the hun-
dred most important books of world history, and yet
whose spiritual life remains as shallow as it ever was, or
perhaps becomes even more superficial. And then look
at an uneducated worker who performs a mechanical
task day by day, but who suddenly asks himself: "What
does it *mean*, that I do this work? What does it mean
for my life? What *is* the meaning of my life?" Because he
asks these questions, that man is on the way into depth,
whereas the other man, the student of history, dwells
on the surface among petrified bodies, brought out of
the depth by some spiritual earthquake of the past. The
simple worker may grasp truth, even though he cannot
answer his questions; the learned scholar may possess
no truth, even though he knows all the truths of the past.

The depth of thought is a part of the depth of life.
Most of our life continues on the surface. We are en-
slaved by the routine of our daily lives, in work and
pleasure, in business and recreation. We are conquered
by innumerable hazards, both good and evil. We are
more driven than driving. We do not stop to look at the
height above us, or to the depth below us. We are always
moving forward, although usually in a circle, which
finally brings us back to the place from which we first
moved. We are in constant motion and never stop to

plunge into the depth. We talk and talk and never listen to the voices speaking to our depth and from our depth. We accept ourselves as we appear to ourselves, and do not care what we really are. Like hit-and-run drivers, we injure our souls by the speed with which we move on the surface; and then we rush away, leaving our bleeding souls alone. We miss, therefore, our depth and our true life. And it is only when the picture that we have of ourselves breaks down completely, only when we find ourselves acting against all the expectations we had derived from that picture, and only when an earthquake shakes and disrupts the surface of our self-knowledge, that we are willing to look into a deeper level of our being.

The wisdom of all ages and of all continents speaks about the road to our depth. It has been described in innumerably different ways. But all those who have been concerned—mystics and priests, poets and philosophers, simple people and educated people—with that road through confession, lonely self-scrutiny, internal or external catastrophes, prayer, contemplation, have witnessed to the same experience. They have found that they were not what they believed themselves to be, even after a deeper level had appeared to them below the vanishing surface. That deeper level itself became surface, when a still deeper level was discovered, this happening again and again, as long as their very lives, as long as they kept on the road to their depth.

Today a new form of this method has become famous, the so-called "psychology of depth". It leads us from the surface of our self-knowledge into levels where things are recorded which we knew nothing about on the surface of our consciousness. It shows us traits of character which contradict everything that we believed we knew about ourselves. It can help us to find the way into our depth, although it cannot help us in an ultimate way, because it cannot guide us to the deepest ground of our being and of all being, the depth of life itself.

The name of this infinite and inexhaustible depth and ground of all being is *God*. That depth is what the word *God* means. And if that word has not much meaning for you, translate it, and speak of the depths of your life, of the source of your being, of your ultimate concern, of what you take seriously without any reservation. Perhaps, in order to do so, you must forget everything traditional that you have learned about God, perhaps even that word itself. For if you know that God means depth, you know much about Him. You cannot then call yourself an atheist or unbeliever. For you cannot think or say: Life has no depth! Life itself is shallow. Being itself is surface only. If you could say this in complete seriousness, you would be an atheist; but otherwise you are not. He who knows about depth knows about God.

We have considered the depth of the world and the depth of our souls. But we are only in a world through a community of men. And we can discover our souls only through the mirror of those who look at us. There is no depth of life without the depth of the common life. We usually live in history as much on the surface as we live our individual lives. We understand our historical existence as it appears to us, and not as it really is. The stream of daily news, the waves of daily propaganda, and the tides of conventions and sensationalism keep our minds occupied. The noise of these shallow waters prevents us from listening to the sounds out of the depth, to the sounds of what really happens in the ground of our social structure, in the longing hearts of the masses, and in the struggling minds of those who

are sensitive to historical changes. Our ears are as deaf
to the cries out of the social depth as they are to the
cries out of the depth of our souls. We leave the bleeding victims of our social system as alone, after we have
hurt them without hearing their cries in the noise of our
daily lives, as we do our own bleeding souls. We believed
once that we were living in a period of unavoidable
progress to a better humanity. But in the depth of our
social structure the forces of destruction had already
gathered strength. It once seemed as if human reason
had conquered nature and history. But this was surface
only; and in the depth of our community the rebellion
against the surface had already begun. We produced
ever better and ever more perfect tools and means for
the life of mankind. But in the depth they had already
turned into means and tools for man's self-destruction.
Decades ago prophetic minds looked into the depth.
Painters expressed their feeling of the coming catastrophe by disrupting the surface of man and of nature
in their pictures. Poets used strange, offensive words and
rhythms in order to throw light upon the contrast between what seemed to be and what really was. Beside
the psychology of depth, a sociology of depth arose.
But it is only now, in the decade in which the most horrible social earthquake of all times has grasped the whole
of mankind, that the eyes of the nations have been
opened to the depth below them and to the truth about
their historical existence. Yet still there are people, even
in high places, who turn their eyes from this depth, and
who wish to return to the disrupted surface as though
nothing had happened. But we who know the depth of
what has happened should not be content to rest upon
the level that we have reached. We might become despairing and self-despising. Let us rather plunge more

deeply into the ground of our historical life, into the ultimate depth of history. The name of this infinite and inexhaustible ground of history is *God*. That is what the word means, and it is that to which the words *Kingdom of God* and *Divine Providence* point. And if these words do not have much meaning for you, translate them, and speak of the depth of history, of the ground and aim of our social life, and of what you take seriously without reservation in your moral and political activities. Perhaps you should call this depth *hope*, simply hope. For if you find hope in the ground of history, you are united with the great prophets who were able to look into the depth of their times, who tried to escape it, because they could not stand the horror of their visions, and who yet had the strength to look to an even deeper level and there to discover hope. Their hope did not make them feel ashamed. And no hope shall make us ashamed, if we do not find it on the surface where fools cultivate vain expectations, but rather if we find it in the depth where those with trembling and contrite hearts receive the strength of a hope which is truth.

These last words shall lead us to the other meaning that the words "deep" and "depth" have in both secular and religious language: the depth of suffering which is the door, the only door, to the depth of truth. That fact is obvious. It is comfortable to live on the surface so long as it remains unshaken. It is painful to break away from it and to descend into an unknown ground. The tremendous amount of resistance against that act in every human being and the many pretexts invented to avoid the road into the depth are natural. The pain of looking into one's own depth is too intense for most people. They would rather return to the shaken and devastated surface of their former lives and thoughts.

The same is true of social groups who create all kinds of ideologies and rationalizations in order to resist those who would lead them to the road to the depth of their social existence. They would rather cover the breaches in their surface with small remedies than to dig into the ground. The prophets of all time can tell us of the hating resistance which they provoke by their daring to uncover the depths of social judgment and social hope. And who can really bear the ultimate depth, the burning fire in the ground of all being, without saying with the prophet, "Woe unto me! For I am undone. For mine eyes have seen the Lord of Hosts!"

Our attempt to avoid the road which leads to such a depth of suffering and our use of pretexts to avoid it are natural. One of the methods, and a very superficial one, is the assertion that deep things are sophisticated things, unintelligible to an uneducated mind. But the mark of real depth is its simplicity. If you should say, "This is too profound for me; I cannot grasp it", you are self-deceptive. For you ought to know that nothing of real importance is too profound for anyone. It is not because it is too profound, but rather because it is too uncomfortable, that you shy away from the truth. Let us not confuse the sophisticated things with the deep things of life. The sophisticated things do not concern us ultimately· and it does not matter whether we understand them or not. But the deep things must concern us always, because it matters infinitely whether we are grasped by them or not.

There is a more serious fact about the road to the depth which can be used as an excuse by those who wish to avoid it. The depth in religious language is often used to express the dwelling place of the evil forces, of the daemonic powers, of death and hell. Is not the

road into the depth a road into the realm which is controlled by these forces? Are there not the elements of
destructiveness and morbidity in the longing for depth?
When an American friend of mine expressed to a group
of German refugees his admiration of the German
depth, we asked ourselves whether we could accept
that praise. Was not that depth the soil out of which
the most daemonic forces of modern history sprang?
Was not that depth a morbid and destructive depth?
Let me answer these questions by telling you and old
and beautiful myth: when the soul leaves the body, it
must pass over many spheres where daemonic forces
rule; and only the soul that knows the right and powerful word can continue its way to the ultimate depth of
the Divine Ground. No soul can avoid these tests. If we
consider the battles of the saints of all times, of the
prophets and the reformers, and of the great creators
in all realms, we can recognize the truth of that myth.
Everyone has to face the deep things of life. That there
is danger is no excuse. The danger must be conquered
by knowledge of the liberating word. The German people and many people in all nations did not know the
word, and therefore, missing the ultimate and saving
depth, were caught by the evil forces of the depth.

There is no excuse which permits us to avoid the depth
of truth, the only way to which lies through the depth
of suffering. Whether the suffering comes from outside
and we take it upon ourselves as the road to the depth,
or whether it be chosen voluntarily as the only way to
deep things; whether it be the way of humility, or the
way of revolution; whether the Cross be internal, or
whether it be external, the road runs contrary to the
way we formerly lived and thought. That is why Isaiah
praises Israel, the Servant of God, in the depths of its

suffering; and why Jesus calls those blessed who are in
the depth of sorrow and persecution, of hunger and
thirst in both body and spirit; and why He demands the
loss of our lives for the sake of our lives. That is why
two great revolutionaries, Thomas Muenzer of the six-
teenth century and Karl Marx of the nineteenth century, speak in similar terms of the vocation of those
who stand at the limits of humanity—in the depths of
emptiness, as Muenzer calls it; in the depth of inhu-
manity, as Marx calls it—those of the proletariat to whom
they pointed as the bearers of a saving future.

And as it is in our lives, so it is in our thought: every
element seems to be reversed. Religion and Christianity
have often been accused of an irrational and paradoxical character. Certainly much stupidity, superstition
and fanaticism have been connected with them. The
command to sacrifice one's intellect is more daemonic
than divine. For man ceases to be man if he ceases to
be an intellect. But the depth of sacrifice, of suffering,
and of the Cross is demanded of our thinking. Every
step into the depth of thought is a breaking away from
the surface of former thoughts. When this breaking
away occurred in men like Paul, Augustine and Luther,
such extreme suffering was involved that it was experienced as death and hell. But they accepted such sufferings as the road to the deep things of God, as the spiritual way, as the way to truth. They expressed the truth
they envisioned in spiritual words—that is, in words
which were contrary to all surface reasoning, but harmonious with the depth of reason, which is divine. The
paradoxical language of religion reveals the way to the
truth as a way to the depth, and therefore as a way of
suffering and sacrifice. He alone who is willing to go
that way is able to understand the paradoxes of religion.

The last thing I want to say about the way to the depth concerns one of these paradoxes. The end of the way is joy. And joy is deeper than suffering. It is ultimate. Let me express this in the words of a man who, in passionate striving for the depth, was caught by destructive forces and did not know the word to conquer them. Friedrich Nietzsche writes: "The world is deep, and deeper than the day could read. Deep is its woe. Joy deeper still than grief can be. Woe says: Hence, go! But joys want all eternity, want deep, profound eternity."

Eternal joy is the end of the ways of God. This is the message of all religions. The Kingdom of God is peace and joy. This is the message of Christianity. But eternal joy is not to be reached by living on the surface. It is rather attained by breaking through the surface, by penetrating the deep things of ourselves, of our world, and of God. The moment in which we reach the last depth of our lives is the moment in which we can experience the joy that has eternity within it, the hope that cannot be destroyed, and the truth on which life and death are built. For in the depth is truth; and in the depth is hope; and in the depth is joy.

8

ON THE TRANSITORINESS OF LIFE

Lord, thou hast been our dwelling place
Age after age.
Before the mountains were born
And earth and land labored in pains of birth.
From eternity to eternity thou art God.
For a thousand years in thy sight
Are but as yesterday when it is passed.
Thou turnest man back to dust
And sayest: Return, ye children of man.
They are as a watch in the night;
Thou carriest them away;
They are as a sleep,
Like grass which grows up,
That in the dawn is fresh and flourishing,
Then by twilight fades and withers.
Our life is seventy years
Or eighty at the most.
Yet is their pride
But toil and disappointment—
For it is soon gone and we fly away.
For we are consumed in thy anger
And in thy wrath we are frightened away.
Thou hast set our iniquities before thee

*And our most secret deeds in the light of thy coun-
    tenance.
For all our days are passed away in thy wrath,
We bring our years to an end as a sigh.
Yet who knoweth the power of thine anger
And who of us dreads thy wrath?
So teach us to count our days
That we may get a heart of wisdom!*

*Relent, O thou Eternal, and delay not;
Be sorry for thy servants.
Satisfy us in the morning with thy loving-kindness
That we may rejoice and be glad all our days.
Grant joy as long as thou hast been afflicting us,
For all the years we have had suffering.
Let thy work appear unto thy servants
And thy glory upon thy children!
And let the favor of the Lord our God be upon us
And prosper the work of our hands!*

PSALM 90.

THERE IS SOMETHING UNIQUE IN THIS
psalm, a rise and fall of praise and lament, of consideration and prayer, of melancholy and hope. If we want to
grasp its meaning, we must follow it, word by word, feeling what the poet has felt, trying to see what he has seen,
looking at our own life through his vision, as it is interpreted through his mighty words. These words come to
us from the furthest past, yet they speak to our present
and to every future. Later generations in Israel expressed

their feeling for the incomparable power of this psalm by attributing it—and it alone—to Moses, whom they called the man of God. Let us approach it with the same awe. This psalm, like many other passages of the Bible, speaks of man's life and death in profoundly pessimistic words. It echoes what God said to Adam in the third chapter of Genesis: "Cursed is the land for thy sake. In toil shalt thou eat of it all the days of thy life. . . . In the sweat of thy face shalt thou eat bread till thou return unto the ground; for out it wast thou taken: for dust thou art, and unto dust shalt thou return." It would be hard to intensify the melancholy of these words. And it would be hard for a modern pessimist to intensify the bitterness with which Job challenges his moralistic friends, saying that "man born of woman lives but a few days", that there is hope for a tree which is cut off, that it may flourish again, but "man lies down never to arise." And he says to God: "Thou destroyest all the hopes of man. Thou art too strong for him, he has to go." And the modern naturalist would need to change nothing in the words of Ecclesiastes, the "Preacher", when he denies that there is any difference between man and beast: "As one dies the other dies. Both sprang from the dust and to the dust they both return." He doubts the idealistic doctrine that "the spirit of man goes upward while the spirit of a beast goes down into the earth." Man ought to be happy in his work, for "that is what he gets out of life—for who can show him what is to happen afterward?"

That is the mood of ancient mankind. Many of us are afraid of it. A shallow Christian idealism cannot stand the darkness of such a vision. Not so the Bible. The most universal of all books, it reveals the age-old wisdom about man's transitoriness and misery. The Bible does not try to hide the truth about man's life under facile statements about the immortality of the soul. Neither the Old nor the New Testament does so. They know the human situation and they take it seriously. They do not give us any easy comfort about ourselves.

This is the light in which we must read the 90th Psalm. But the psalm goes further. It starts with a song of praise: "Lord, thou hast been our dwelling place age after age." In order to describe human transitoriness, the poet glorifies the Divine Eternity. Before looking downward he looks upward. Before considering man's misery he points to God's majesty. Only because we look at something infinite can we realize that we are finite. Only because we are able to see the eternal can we see the limited time that is given us. Only because we can elevate ourselves above the animals can we see that we are like animals. Our melancholy about our transitoriness is rooted in our power to look beyond it. Modern pessimists do not start their writings by praising the Eternal God. They think that they can approach man directly and speak about his finiteness, misery and tragedy. But they do not succeed. Hidden—often to themselves—is a criterion by which they measure and condemn human existence. It is something beyond man. When the Greek poets called men the "mortals", they had in mind the immortal gods by which they measured human mortality. The measure of man's transitoriness is God's eternity; the measure of man's misery and tragedy is the Divine Perfection. That is what the psalmist means when he calls God our dwelling place, the only permanence in the change of all the ages and generations. That is why he starts his song of profoundest melancholy with the praise of the Lord.

God's eternity is described in a powerful vision: "Be-

fore the mountains were born and earth and land labored in pains of birth, from eternity to eternity thou
art God." Even the mountains, most immovable of all
things on earth, are born and shall die. But God, Who
was before their birth, *shall be* after their death. From
eternity to eternity, that is, from form to form and world
to world, He *is*. His measure of time is not our measure.
"For a thousand years in thy sight are but as yesterday
when it is passed." He has His measure, which is beyond
human understanding. Eternity is not the extinction of
time; it is the creative unity of all times and cycles of
time, of all past and future. Eternity is eternal life and
not eternal death. It is the living God at Whom the
psalmist looks.

And then the psalmist looks down to man and writes:
"Thou turnest man back to dust and sayest: Return, ye
children of man." The fate of death is the fate God has
decreed for man. God delivers us to the law of nature,
that dust must return to dust. No being can escape this
decree. No being can acquire Divine eternity. When
man tried to become like God—so the Paradise story
tells us—by trying to grasp for himself knowledge of all
good and evil powers, he achieved that knowledge. But,
at the same time, his eyes were opened and he saw his
real situation, which had been hidden from him in the
dreaming innocence of Paradise. He saw that he is not
like God. The gift of knowledge he received includes
the destiny of sex and the fate of laboring and dying.
He was awakened and he saw the infinite gap between
himself and God.

Short is the time between birth and death. The poet's
tremendous vision is expressed only fragmentarily, in
similes: "They are as a watch in the night", that is, like
one of the three night watches into which the nights

were divided. "Thou carriest them away, they are as a sleep"—from an infinite sleep we are awakened; one third of a night we are awake, this is our turn, this long and no longer; soon those who replace us arrive, and we are drawn into infinite sleep again. Turning from the night to the course of a day, and the life of the grass in it, the poet continues: "Like grass which grows up, that in the dawn is fresh and flourishing, then by twilight fades and withers." The sun, whose first rays bring life to the grass, burns it to death at noon and withers it utterly away before evening. So short is our life— and it seems so long. "Our life is seventy years, or eighty at the most, yet is their pride—but toil and disappointment . . . for it is soon gone and we fly away." Not many reach this age, which seems unimaginable to the adolescent, far removed from the mature man, and—as nothing to those who have reached it, a moment only, flying away like a bird that we can neither capture nor follow.

Why is the poet so tremendously impressed by the shortness of our life? Obviously, he feels that it makes a real fulfillment impossible. Although very few want to repeat their lives, we often hear people say: "If only I could start my life again, with all its experiences, I could live it in the right way. It would be more than this broken piece, this fragment, this frustrated attempt which I call my life." But life does not allow us to begin again. And even if we could begin again, or even if our life were among the most perfect and happy and successful ones, would we not, looking back at it, feel as the psalmist felt? Would we not feel that the most valuable things in it, the good, the creative, and the joyful hours, were based on endless toil and followed by disappointment? Would we not feel that what we had thought to be important was not? And, in the face of death, would not all our valuations become doubtful? This, certainly, was the mood of the ancient poet who wrote the psalm.

There is a danger in considerations such as these. They can produce a sentimental, superficial enjoyment of our own melancholy, a lustful abiding with our sadness, a perverted longing for the tragic. There is not a hint of such a feeling in the 90th Psalm. The poet knew something which most of our modern pessimists do not know, and he expresses it in grave words: "For we are condemned in thy anger, and in thy wrath we are frightened away. Thou hast set our iniquities before thee and our most secret deeds in the light of thy countenance." These words point to something we do not find in nature: man's guilt and God's wrath. Another order of things becomes visible. The natural law "from dust to dust" alone does not explain the human situation. That man is bound to this law is the Divine reaction against the attempt of man to become like God. We have to die, because we are dust. That is the law of nature to which we are subject with all beings—mountains, flowers, and beasts. But, at the same time, we have to die because we are guilty. That is the moral law to which we, unlike all other beings, are subject. Both laws are equally true; both are stated in all sections of the Bible. If we could ask the psalmist or the other Biblical writers how they thought these laws are united, they would find it hard to answer. They felt, as we do, that death is not only natural, but also unnatural. Something in us rebels against death wherever it appears. We rebel at the sight of a corpse, we rebel against the death of children, of young people, of men and women in their strength. We even feel a tragic element in the passing of old people, with their experience, wisdom, and irreplaceable individuality. We rebel against our own end, against its definitive, inescapable character. We would not rebel if death were simply natural, as we do not rebel against the falling of the leaves. We accept their falling, although we do so with melancholy. But we do not accept man's death in the same way. We rebel; and since our rebellion is useless, we become resigned. Between rebellion against death and resignation to death we oscillate, demonstrating by both attitudes that it is not natural for us to die.

Death is the work of the Divine wrath: "For all our days are passed away in thy wrath, we bring our years to an end as a sigh"—as short as a sigh, and as full of sorrow as a sigh. The idea of the Divine wrath has become strange to our time. We have rejected a religion which seemed to make God a furious tyrant, an individual with passions and desires who committed arbitrary acts. This is not what the wrath of God means. It means the inescapable and unavoidable reaction against every distortion of the law of life, and above all against human pride and arrogance. That reaction, through which man is thrown back into his limits, is not a passionate act of punishment or vengeance on the part of God. It is the reëstablishment of the balance between God and man, which is disturbed by man's elevation against God.

The poet expresses his profound understanding of the relation between God and man in the statement that God sets our innermost secrets in the light of His face. God's anger is not directed against our moral shortcomings, against special acts of disobedience to the Divine order. It is directed against the secret of our personality, against what happens in us and to us, unseen by men, unseen even by ourselves. This, our secret, determines our fate, more than anything visible. In the realm of our visible deeds we may not feel that we deserve the wrath of God—misery and tragedy. But God looks through the veils which hide our secrets. They are manifest to Him. Therefore, we feel every day the burden of being under a power which negates us, which disintegrates us and makes us unhappy. This is the wrath under which we pass all our days, not only those in which we endure special failures and special sufferings.

This is the situation of all men. But not all men know it. "Yet who knoweth the power of thine anger, and who of us dreads thy wrath? So teach us to count our days, that we may get a heart of wisdom!" The 90th Psalm tries to teach us the truth about our human situation, our transitoriness and our guilt. It does what the great ancient tragedies did. They revealed to all the people of the city, gathered in the theatre, what man is; they showed the people that the greatest, the best, the most beautiful, the most powerful—all—stand under the tragic law and the curse of the immortals. They wanted to reveal the tragic situation of man, that is, his situation before the Divine. He becomes great and proud and tries to touch the Divine sphere, and he is cast into destruction and despair. This is what the psalmist wanted to reveal to the righteous and unrighteous people of his nation—what they were; what man is.

But the psalmist knew that men, even if shaken for a moment, forgot their fate. He knew that men live as if they are to live forever, and as if the wrath of God did not exist. Therefore, he asks us to count our days, to consider how soon they shall come to an end. He prays God that He Himself may teach us that we must die.

The psalmist does not think that realization of the

truth of what he has been saying will cast man into
despair. On the contrary, he believes that just this insight can give us a heart of wisdom—a heart which accepts the infinite distance between God and man, and
does not claim a greatness and beatitude which belongs
to God alone.

The wise heart is the heart which does not try to hide
this from itself, which does not try to escape into a false
security or a false cynicism. The wise heart is the heart
which can stand this knowledge courageously, with dignity, humility, and fortitude. This wisdom is implicit
in every word of the psalm. It is the greatest wisdom that
man, having felt the tragedy of life, achieved in the
ancient world.

After the prayer for the wise heart (and not for intellectual wisdom!) a new section of the psalm begins,
perhaps added in a later period of the Jewish religion.
This new section is concerned with the nation and its
historical situation. "Relent, O Thou Eternal, and delay
not, be sorry for thy servants. Satisfy us in the morning with thy loving-kindness, that we may rejoice and be
glad all our days. Grant joy as long as thou hast been
afflicting us, for all the years we have had suffering. Let
thy work appear unto thy servants and thy glory upon
thy children! And let the favor of the Lord our God be
upon us and prosper the work of our hands!" Something
new appears in these words: the significance of past and
future, the prayer for a better future, for a future of
happiness and joy, of the presence of God and the suc-
cess of our work. God is not only the God of eternity. He
is also the God of the future. The cycle from dust to
dust, from sin to wrath, is broken. There appears the
vision of an age of fulfillment, after the ages of misery.
But this vision is only for His servants—for the selected

74   *The Shaking of the Foundations*

nation, and within her, only for those who are really
His servants. The individual no longer stands alone be
fore God. He is included among the other servants of
God, in the midst of the people of God who look not
toward their return to dust, but toward a life in a new
age in which God is present. Hope supersedes tragedy.
This is the highest point that religion reaches in the
Old Testament.

But the spirit of religion drives beyond even this. It
is not the end. What does the historical hope mean for
the individual? Does it free us from the law of transitoriness and guilt? History, running toward the unknown
future, throws every man back into the past, and we
do not reach the age of fulfillment for which the poet
longs. The cruel step of history goes over our graves,
and history itself does not seem to approach its fulfillment. Whenever history seems to come near to its fulfillment, it is thrown back and is farther away from its
fulfillment than ever before. That is what we experience
so inescapably in our time. And so we ask, as all generations of men have asked: is tragedy stronger than hope?
Does the past conquer the future? Is wrath more powerful than mercy? We are driven to and fro between melancholy and expectation—from tragedy to hope, from
hope to tragedy. In this situation we may be ready to
receive the message of a new being, a new kind of existence which is not only hope, but also reality, in which
Divine wrath and human guilt ultimately are conquered. Christianity is based on this message: God sub-
jecting Himself to transitoriness and wrath, in order to
be with us. And thus is fulfilled the hope of which the
psalmist sings: "Let thy work appear unto thy servants
and thy glory upon thy children."

Whether or not we accept that message, it is the

answer to the questions the psalmist leaves unanswered. We may prefer to cling to the mere hope in spite of all disillusionments. We may prefer to return to the pious resignation of the older part of the psalm. We may even prefer to go back to the melancholic identification of man's life with that of the grass of the field. We may choose any of these ways of interpreting our life. But if we do choose any of them, we must realize that we cannot find in them the answer to the question of our life. And we must be resigned. But if we accept the message of the new reality in the Christ, we must understand that this message does not contain an easy answer, and that it does not guarantee any spiritual security. We must know that it is a real answer only if we understand it permanently in the light of our human situation, in which tragedy and hope fight each other without victory. The victory is above them. The victory came when the prayer of the psalmist was answered. "Relent, O thou Eternal!"—this prayer is the prayer of mankind through all eons, and the hidden prayer in the depth of every human soul.

9

"NATURE, ALSO, MOURNS FOR A LOST GOOD"

Day unto day uttereth speech,
And night unto night sheweth knowledge.
There is no speech nor language,
Where their voice is not heard.
Their line is gone out through all the earth,
And their words to the end of the world.
In them hath he set a tabernacle for the sun,
Which is as a bridegroom coming out of his chamber,
And rejoiceth as a strong man to run a race.

PSALM 19:2-5.

For the earnest expectation of the creature wait-
eth for the manifestation of the sons of God. For the
creature was made subject to vanity, not willingly,
but by reason of him who hath subjected the same
in hope, because the creature itself also shall be
delivered from the bondage of corruption into the
glorious liberty of the children of God. For we know
that the whole creation groaneth and travaileth in
pain together until now. ROMANS 8:19-22.

And I saw a new heaven and a new earth: for the
first heaven and the first earth were passed away; and
there was no more sea. . . . And he shewed me a

pure river of water of life, clear as crystal, proceeding out of the throne of God and of the Lamb. In the midst of the street of it, and on either side of the river, was there the tree of life, which bare twelve manner of fruits, and yielded her fruit every month: and the leaves of the tree were for the healing of the nations. REVELATION 21:1; 22:1-2.

EACH YEAR WHEN GOOD FRIDAY AND Easter Sunday approach us our thoughts turn toward the great drama of redemption, culminating in the pictures of the Cross and Resurrection. Who is redeemed? Some men alone; or mankind, including all nations; or the world, everything that is created, including nature, the stars and the clouds, the winds and the oceans, the stones and the plants, the animals and our own bodies? The Bible speaks again and again of the salvation of the *world,* as it speaks of the creation of the *world* and the subjection of the *world* to anti-Divine forces. And *world* means nature as well as man.

So let us ask today: what does nature mean to us? What does it mean to itself? What does it mean in the great drama of creation and salvation? A threefold answer is contained in the words of the psalmist, the apostle and the prophet: the psalmist sings of the glory of nature; the apostle shows the tragedy of nature; and the prophet pronounces the salvation of nature. The hymn of the psalmist praises the glory of God in the glory of nature; the letter of the apostle links the tragedy of nature to the tragedy of man; and the vision of the prophet sees the salvation of nature in the salvation of the world.

So let us listen once more to the words of the psalm-ist, about the glory of nature, in their precise meaning.

The heavens are telling the glory of God,
And the firmament showeth the work of his hands.
Day unto day poureth forth the story,
Night unto night announces the knowledge.
There is no speech, no language!
Their voice cannot be heard!
But their music goes out through all the earth,
And their words to the end of the world.

The 19th Psalm points to an old belief held by the ancient world and expressed by poets and philosophers: that the heavenly bodies, the sun and the moon and the stars, produce by their movement a harmony of tones, sounding day and night from one end of the world to the other. These voices of the universe are not heard by human ears; they do not speak in human language. But they exist, and we can perceive them through the organs of our spirit. Shakespeare says:

There's not the smallest orb which thou behold'st,
But in his motion like an angel sings. . . .
Such harmony is in immortal souls;
But whilst this muddy vesture of decay
Doth grossly close it in, we cannot hear it. . . .*

The psalmist *has* heard it; he knows what the stars are sounding: the glory of creation and its Divine Ground.

Are *we* able to perceive the hidden voice of nature? Does nature speak to us? Does it speak to you? Or has nature become silent to us, silent to the men of our period? Some of you may say, "Never before in any period has nature been so open to man as it is today. The mysteries of the past have become the knowledge of

---

* *The Merchant of Venice*, V. sc. 1.

children. Through every scientific book, through every laboratory, through every machine, nature speaks to us. The technical use of nature is the revelation of its mystery." The voice of nature *has* been heard by the scientific mind, and its answer is the conquest of nature. But is this all that nature says to us?

I was sitting under a tree with a great biologist. Suddenly he exclaimed, "I would like to know something about this tree!" He, of course, knew everything that science had to say about it. I asked him what he meant. And he answered, "I want to know what this tree means for itself. I want to understand the life of this tree. It is so strange, so unapproachable." He longed for a sympathetic understanding of the *life* of nature. But such an understanding is possible only by communion between man and nature. Is such communion possible in our period of history? Is nature not completely subjected to the will and wilfulness of man? This technical civilization, the pride of mankind, has brought about a tremendous devastation of original nature, of the land, of animals, of plants. It has kept genuine nature in small reservations and has occupied everything for domination and ruthless exploitation. And worse: many of us have lost the ability to live with nature. We fill it with the noise of empty talk, instead of listening to its many voices, and, through them, to the voiceless music of the universe. Separated from the soil by a machine, we speed through nature, catching glimpses of it, but never comprehending its greatness or feeling its power. Who is still able to penetrate, meditating and contemplating, the creative ground of nature? A Chinese emperor asked a famous painter to paint a picture of a rooster for him. The painter assented, but said that it would take a long time. After a year the emperor reminded him of his promise. The painter replied that after a year of study-

ing the rooster he had just begun to perceive the surface
of its nature. After another year the artist asserted that
he had just begun to penetrate the essence of this kind
of life. And so on, year after year. Finally, after ten
years of concentration on the nature of the rooster, he
painted the picture—a work described as an inexhaustible revelation of the divine ground of the universe in
one small part of it, a rooster. Compare the emperor's
wise patience and the painter's saintly contemplation of
an infinitely small expression of the divine life, with the
exuberances of our contemporaries, who rush in their
cars to some famous view and exclaim, "How lovely!"
—referring, no doubt, not to the view, but to their own
appreciation of beauty. What blasphemy of the glory
of nature! and consequently of the divine ground, the
glory of which sounds through the glory of nature.

Praising the glory of nature does not mean speaking
of the beauty of nature alone and forgetting its overwhelming greatness and terrible power. Nature never
manifests shallow beauty or merely obvious harmony.
"The voice of the Lord is powerful", sings the poet of
the 29th Psalm. "The voice of the Lord breaketh the
cedars . . . the voice of the Lord cleaveth with flames
of fire, the voice of the Lord shaketh the wilderness
. . . and strippeth the forests bare." In the book of Job,
we find a description of the terrible power of nature
in the mythological symbols of Behemoth and Levia-
than. And a great recent poet, Rilke, says:

> . . . For Beauty's nothing
> but beginning of Terror we're still just able to bear,
> and why we adore it so is because it serenely
> disdains to destroy us. Each single angel is terrible.

The glory of nature is not shallow beauty.

And now let us listen once more to the words of the apostle about the tragedy of nature in their precise meaning.

> Even the creation waits with eager longing for the sons of God to be revealed. For creation was not rendered futile by its own choice, but by the will of Him Who thus made it subject, the hope being that creation as well as man would one day be freed from its thraldom to decay and gain the glorious freedom of God's children. To this day, we know, the entire creation sighs and throbs with pain.*

Nature is not only glorious; it is also tragic. It is subjected to the laws of finitude and destruction. It is suffering and sighing with us. No one who has ever listened to the sounds of nature with sympathy can forget their tragic melodies. The Greek word in Paul's letter which we have translated as "creation" is especially used for the non-animated section of nature as Paul is alluding to the words of God to Adam after the Fall: "Cursed is the land for thy sake." The sighing sounds of the wind and the ever-restless, futile breaking of the waves may have inspired the poetic, melancholic verse about nature's subjection to vanity. But the words of Paul refer also, and in a more direct way, to the sphere of living things. The melancholy of the leaves falling in autumn, the end of the jubilant life of spring and summer, the quiet death of innumerable beings in the cold air of the approaching winter—all this has grasped and always will grasp the hearts, not only of poets, but of every feeling man and woman. The song of transitoriness sounds

* Romans 8:19-22.

through all the nations. Isaiah's words, "The grass withereth, the flower fadeth, because the breath of the Lord bloweth upon it", describe the shortness of the lives of individuals and nations. But they could not have been written without a profound sympathy with the life of nature. And then Jesus speaks, praising the lilies of the field: "Even Solomon in all his glory was not arrayed like one of these." In these two sayings about the flowers of the field we perceive both the glory and the tragedy of nature.

Sympathy with nature in its tragedy is not a sentimental emotion; it is a true feeling of the reality of nature. Schelling justly says: "A veil of sadness is spread over all nature, a deep, unappeasable melancholy over all life." According to him this is "manifest through the traces of suffering in the face of all nature, especially in the faces of the animals." The doctrine of suffering as the character of all life, taught by the Buddha, has conquered large sections of mankind. But only he who is connected in the ground of his own being with the ground of nature is able to see into its tragedy; as Schelling says, "The darkest and deepest ground in human nature is 'Longing' . . . is melancholy. This, mainly, creates the sympathy of man with nature. For in nature too the deepest ground is melancholy. Nature, also, mourns for a lost good." Can we still understand the meaning of such half-poetic, half-philosophic words? Or have we too much secluded ourselves in human superiority, in intellectual arrogance, in a domineering attitude toward nature? We have become incapable of perceiving the harmonious sounds of nature. Have we also become insensitive to the tragic sounds?

Why is nature tragic? Who is responsible for the suffering of animals, for the ugliness of death and decay,

for the universal dread of death? Many years ago I stood
on a jetty with a well-known psychologist looking at the
ocean. We saw innumerable small fish hurrying toward
the beach. They were pursued by bigger ones, who, in
turn, were chased by still bigger ones. Aggression, flight,
and anxiety—a perfect illustration of the old, often used
story of the big fish devouring the small ones, in nature
as in history. The scholar, who, in many discussions,
had defended the harmonious structure of reality, burst
into tears, saying, "Why are these beings created if they
exist only to be swallowed by others?" In this moment
the tragedy of nature forced itself upon his optimistic
mind, and he asked, "Why?"

Paul tries to penetrate the mystery of this question.
And his surprising answer is: nature is subjected to
vanity by the curse that God uttered because of the
fall of Adam. The tragedy of nature is bound to the
tragedy of man, as the salvation of nature is dependent
on the salvation of man. What does this mean? Always
mankind has dreamed of a time when harmony and joy
filled all nature, and peace reigned between nature and
man—Paradise, the Golden Age. But man, by violating
the divine law, destroyed the harmony, and now there
is enmity between man and nature, between nature and
nature. In Paul's melancholic words this dream resounds.
It is a dream, but it contains a profound truth: man
and nature belong together in their created glory, in
their tragedy, and in their salvation. As nature, repre-
sented by the "Serpent", leads man into temptation, so
man, by his trespassing of the divine law, leads nature
into tragedy. This did not happen once upon a time, as
the story says; it happens within every time and space,
as long as there is time and space. So long as there are
the old heaven and the old earth, man and nature will

be subjected together to the law of vanity. Many profound thinkers within and without Christianity agree that man is determined to fulfill the longing of nature. In so far as he has failed and still fails to come to his own fulfillment, he is unable to fulfill nature—his own bodily being and nature around him. Therefore, Jesus is called the Son of Man, the man from above, the true man, in whom the forces of separation and tragedy are overcome, not only in mankind but also in the universe. For there is no salvation of man if there is no salvation of nature, for man is in nature and nature is in man.

Let us listen once more to the words of the prophet about the salvation of nature.

> Then I saw the new heaven and the new earth. For the first heaven and the first earth had passed away; and the sea was no more. . . . Then he showed me the river of the water of life, bright as crystal . . . on both sides of the river grew the tree of life, bearing twelve kinds of fruit, each month having its own fruit; and the leaves of the tree were for the healing of the nations.*

In powerful images the last book of the Bible describes the salvation of man and nature from the bondage of corruption: the city of God is built with the most precious materials of non-animated nature. The ocean, the symbol of formless chaos, is excluded. The river is not polluted by any rot. The trees bear fruit without change and decay; the animals, together with the saints, adore the throne of glory. The daemonic forces are thrown into nothingness. There is no suffering nor death.

Needless to say, this is not the description of a future

---

* Rev. 21:1, 22:2.

state of our world. Like the Golden Age of the past, the Golden Age of the future is a symbol, pointing to something mysterious within our present world—namely, the forces of salvation. And one thing is made very clear in the visions of the prophet, that salvation means salvation of the *world,* and not of human beings alone. Lions and sheep, little children and snakes, will lie together in peace, says Isaiah. Angels and stars, men and animals, adore the Child of the Christmas legend. The earth shakes when the Christ dies, and it shakes again when He is resurrected. The sun loses its light when He closes His eyes, and it rises when He rises from the tomb. The resurrection of the *body*—not an immortal soul—is the symbol of the victory over death. The bodiless spirit (and this is the meaning of all these images) is not the aim of creation; the purpose of salvation is not the abstract intellect or a natureless moral personality. Do we not see everywhere the estrangement of people from nature, from their own natural forces and from nature around them? And do they not become dry and uncreative in their mental life, hard and arrogant in their moral attitude, suppressed and poisoned in their vitality? They certainly are not the images of salvation. As one theologian has justly said, "Corporal being is the end of the ways of God."

This has always been known to creative painters and sculptors. A great picture or statue is an anticipation of the new earth, a revelation of the mystery of nature. A picture or a statue is a plant or a stone transformed into a bearer of spiritual meaning. It is nature elevated above itself, revealing its tragedy and, at the same time, its victory over its tragedy. The picture of Jesus and the apostles and saints throughout the centuries of Christian art, in color and stone—portraits of the men in whom humanity discovered its power and dignity—the incomparable expression of personality in the face of even the simplest individual, show that spirit becomes body, and that nature is not strange to personality. The system of cells and functions, which we call "body," is able to express the finest change of our spiritual being. Artists have often understood the eternal significance of nature, even when theologians have emphasized a bodiless spirituality, forgetting that the first thing by which Jesus revealed His Messianic vocation was His power to heal bodily and mental sickness.

Let me ask you a question: are we still able to understand what a sacrament means? The more we are estranged from nature, the less we can answer affirmatively. That is why, in our time, the sacraments have lost so much of their significance for individuals and Churches. For in the sacraments nature participates in the process of salvation. Bread and wine, water and light, and all the great elements of nature become the bearers of spiritual meaning and saving power. Natural and spiritual powers are united—reunited—in the sacrament. The word appeals to our intellect and may move our will. The sacrament, if its meaning is alive, grasps our unconscious as well as our conscious being. It grasps the creative ground of our being. It is the symbol of nature and spirit, united in salvation.

Therefore, commune with nature! Become reconciled with nature after your estrangement from it. Listen to nature in quietness, and you will find its heart. It will sound forth the glory of its divine ground. It will sigh with us in the bondage of tragedy. It will speak of the indestructible hope of salvation!

10

THE EXPERIENCE OF THE HOLY

In the year that King Uzziah died,
I saw also the Lord sitting upon a throne,
High and lifted up, and his train filled the temple.
Above it stood the seraphims: each one had six wings,
With twain he covered his face,
And with twain he covered his feet,
And with twain he did fly.
And one cried unto another, and said,
Holy, holy holy, is the Lord of hosts:
The whole earth is full of his glory.
And the posts of the door moved at the voice of him
*   that cried,*
And the house was filled with smoke.
Then said I, Woe is me! for I am undone;
Because I am a man of unclean lips,
And I dwell in the midst of a people of unclean lips;
For mine eyes have seen the King, the Lord of hosts.
Then flew one of the seraphims unto me, having a
*   live coal in his hand,*
Which he had taken with the tongs from off the altar:
And he laid it upon my mouth, and said,
Lo, this hath touched thy lips;
And thine iniquity is taken away, and thy sin purged
Also I heard the voice of the Lord, saying,

Whom shall I send, and who will go for us?
Then said I, Here am I; send me.
And he said, Go, and tell this people,
Hear ye indeed, but understand not;
And see ye indeed, but perceive not.
Make the heart of this people fat,
And make their ears heavy, and shut their eyes;
Lest they see with their eyes, and hear with their
*   ears,*
And understand with their heart, and convert, and
*   be healed.*
Then said I, Lord, how long? And he answered,
Until the cities be wasted without inhabitant,
And the houses without man,
And the land be utterly desolate.
And the Lord have removed men far away,
And there be a great forsaking in the midst of the
*   land.*
But yet in it shall be a tenth,
And it shall return, and shall be eaten:
As a teil tree, and as an oak,
Whose substance is in them, when they cast their
*   leaves:*
So the holy seed shall be the substance thereof.

ISAIAH 6.

THIS CHAPTER IS ONE OF THE
greatest in the Old Testament. It clearly reveals the
essence of Biblical religion. The prophet describes the
vision of his vocation in words and pictures which ex-

press at the same time his fundamental experience of God, his interpretation of human existence, and his conception of the prophet's task. His experience of God is an experience of the holiness of God. He interprets man's condition as one of uncleanness and inability to face God. The prophet's task is paradoxically set against the natural meaning of prophecy. These three ideas belong together and comprise perhaps the highest expression ever given to the prophetic spirit.

The prophet does not describe God Himself in any way. He speaks only of the train which filled the temple, of the angels surrounding the Lord's throne, of the shaking of the foundation, and of the smoke filling the house. In this manner he indicates that the revelation of God is at the same time the veiling of God. God can reveal Himself only by remaining veiled. But even the veiled revelation makes Isaiah feel that he is perishing. The facing of God, even if it be a mere approaching to His sphere, even if God Himself remain hidden, means the annihilation of man.

The same feeling is expressed in the cry of the seraphim "Holy" has a double meaning, as the context clearly shows. It means the majesty of which the world is full; and it means purity as against human impurity. Glory without purity is the character of all pagan gods. And purity without glory is the character of all the humanistic ideas of God. Humanism has transformed the inaccessibility of God into the sublimity of His moral commands. Humanism has forgotten that God's majesty, as experienced by the prophet, implies the shaking of the foundation wherever He appears, and the veil of smoke whenever He shows Himself. When God is identified with an element in human nature, as in humanism, the terrifying and annihilating encounter with majesty be-

comes an impossibility. But "holy" means also moral
perfection, purity, goodness, truth, and justice. God's
glory can fulfill all the world, only because He is holy
in this double sense. The glory of the gods who are not
holy in this double sense can fulfill only one country,
one family or tribe, one nation or state, or one sphere
of human life. Consequently, they do not possess the
truth and justice and purity of the God Who is really
God. They are demons aspiring to holiness, but excluded
from it, because their glory is majesty without purity.
Therefore, let us say, during this time particularly,
"Thou only art holy!"

The prophet confesses that he is a man of unclean
lips, and that he lives in the midst of a people with unclean lips. He emphasizes his lips, because his work is
preaching; but the impurity of his lips symbolizes the
impurity of his entire existence, and of the existence of
individuals and society as a whole. Isaiah exhibits profound insight, when he identifies himself with his unclean people in the very moment that he is made worthy
of his exceptional vision. The difference between mystical and prophetic religion lies in that insight. For even
in the greatest ecstasy, a prophet does not forget the
social group to which he belongs, and its unclean character which he cannot lose. Consequently, the prophetic
ecstasy, as opposed to the mystical ecstasy, is never an
end in itself, but rather the means of receiving the divine
commands which are to be preached to the people.
Isaiah's vision reveals the two conditions for prophetic
existence. The lips of the prophet must first be purified
by fire. He can then hear the Voice of God, the condition for his being sent by God. Nobody can be the
prophet of God through his own strength; and nobody
can absolve himself. Only the power of Divine Holiness,

having touched our existence, can bring us near to God. Something of our existence, sin, iniquity, or uncleanness must be burned away. must be annihilated. Only through such annihilation can God speak to us and through us. But whether or when He speaks to us at all does not depend upon us in any way. Isaiah did not produce either the vision or the purification. He was overcome with terror and awe. And he had to act. For God asks, "Who will go for us?" God waits for the answer. He does not compel. Isaiah's decision to go must be free. Freedom of decision is the second condition for prophetic existence. A prophet must decide whether or not he will dedicate himself to the task. With respect to our fate and vocation we are free; with respect to our relation to God we are powerless. The majesty of God is evident in either case.

The prophet then describes the content of the divine command. "Make the heart of this people fat, and make their ears heavy, and shut their eyes." Our natural moral feelings refuse to accept such a paradox. For if we speak, we wish to make ourselves heard; and when we preach, we wish to convert and to heal. But the prophet accepts the divine command. And when his natural feeling impels him to ask, "How long?" he receives the answer, "Until the cities be wasted without inhabitant, and the houses without man, and the land be utterly desolate!" No hope or promise is expressed. What is the meaning of that paradox? It means that true prophets are the instruments of God in the actualization of His judgment against mankind. They are instruments in so far as the prophetic word always excites the opposition of man with respect to both his vital existence and his moral and religious existence—indeed, particularly with respect to his religious existence. All people desire

false prophets, who, through the glorification of their
gods, glorify their followers and themselves. People
long to be flattered in regard to their desires and virtues,
their religious feeling and social activity, their will to
power and utopian hopes, their knowledge and love,
their family and race, their class and nation. And a false
prophet can always be found to glorify the demon they
worship. But when the voice of the true prophet is
raised, they shut their ears, they contradict his statements, and they ultimately persecute and kill him, because they are not able to receive his message. The order
endures until the prophet's words are fulfilled, and the
cities are destroyed, and the land is made desolate.

We are all eager for the prophetic spirit. We are
anxious to lead the people to a new justice and to a better
social order. We long to save the nations from a threatening doom. But does *our* word, if it be God's word,
have a better effect than that which Isaiah saw in his
vision and experienced in his life? Are we more than
he was? Are our people today less devoted to demons
than his people were? If not, can we expect anything
other than what he was told to expect through his vision?
We must pray for the prophetic spirit which has been
dead for so long in the Churches. And he who feels that
he has been given the prophetic task must fulfill it as
Isaiah did. He must preach the message of a new justice and of a new social order in the name of God and
His honour. But he must expect to be opposed and
persecuted not only by his enemies, but also by his
friends, party, class, and nation. He must expect to be
persecuted to the degree to which his word is the word
of that God Who alone is holy, that God Who alone is
able to create a holy people out of the remnant of every
nation.

11

THE YOKE OF RELIGION

At that time Jesus answered and said, I thank Thee, O Father, Lord of heaven and earth, because thou hast hid these things from the wise and prudent, and hast revealed them unto babes. Even so, Father: for so it seemed good in thy sight. All things are delivered unto me of my Father: and no man knoweth the Son, but the Father; neither knoweth any man the Father, save the Son, and he to whomsoever the Son will reveal him. Come unto me, all ye that labor and are heavy laden, and I will give you rest. Take my yoke upon you, and learn of me; for I am meek and lowly in heart: and ye shall find rest unto your souls. For my yoke is easy, and my burden is light. MATTHEW 11:25-30.

WHEN I WAS OF THE AGE TO RECEIVE confirmation and full membership in the Church, I was told to choose a passage from the Bible as the expression of my personal approach to the Biblical message and to the Christian Church. Every confirmee was obliged to do so, and to recite the passage before the congregation. When I chose the words, "Come unto me all ye that labor and are heavy laden", I was asked with a kind of astonishment and even irony why I had chosen that particular passage. For I was living under happy conditions, and, being only fifteen years old, was without any apparent labor and burden. I could not answer at that time; I felt a little embarrassed, but basically right. And I was right, indeed; every child is right in responding immediately to those words; every adult is right in responding to them in all periods of his life, and under all the conditions of his internal and external history. These words of Jesus are universal, and fit every human being and every human situation. They are simple; they grasp the heart of the primitive as well as that of the profound, disturbing the mind of the wise. Practically every word of Jesus had this character, sharing the difference between Him as the originator and the dependent interpreters, disciples and theologians, saints and preachers. Returning for the first time in my life to the passage of my early choice, I feel just as grasped by it as at that time, but infinitely more embarrassed by its majesty, profundity and inexhaustible meaning. Our task in the face of words like these is obvious: we must point to the ground of their power over our souls; we must explain why, in their emotional force, the force of an ultimate truth is involved; and we must attempt to view our human situation in their light.

Three questions, aroused by the words of Jesus, shall be asked, and the answers implied in His words shall be interpreted. What is the labor and burden from which we can find rest through Him? What is the easy yoke and the light burden which He will put upon us? Why is He and He alone able to give such rest to our souls?

"All ye that labor and are heavy laden. . . .": this is addressed to all men, although not all men feel it in the same way. It is the general human situation to be heavy laden and to labor restlessly under a yoke too hard to be endured. What kind of burden is this? We may think first of the burdens and labors that daily life imposes upon us. But that is not indicated in our text. Jesus does not tell us that He will ease the labors and burdens of life and work. How could He, even if He wanted to? Whether or not we come to Him, the threats of illness or unemployment are not lessened, the weight of our work does not become easier, the fate of being refugee, driven from one country to another, is not changed; the horror of ruins, wounds, and death falling from heaven is not stopped; and the sorrow over the passing of friends or parents or children is not overcome. Jesus cannot and does not promise more pleasure and less pain to those whom He asks to come to Him. On the contrary, sometimes He promises them more pain, more persecution, more threat of death—the "cross", as He calls it. All this is not the burden to which He points.

Nor is it the burden of sin and guilt, as somebody educated in the traditional Christian interpretation of the work of Christ might assume. Nothing like that is indicated in the words of Jesus. Taking upon oneself His easy yoke does not mean taking sin more easily or taking guilt less seriously. He does not tell those who come to Him that their sins are not so important as they seemed to be. He does not give them an easier conscience about their failures and trespasses. On the contrary, He sharpens their conscience to the highest possible degree in practically every one of His words. He condemns sins which the traditional theology of His time did not even consider as sins. This is not the burden to which He points.

The burden He wants to take from us is the burden of religion. It is the yoke of the law, imposed on the people of His time by the religious teachers, the wise

and understanding, as He calls them in our words, the
Scribes and Pharisees, as they are called usually. Those
who labor and are heavy laden are those who are sighing under the yoke of the religious law. And He will
give them the power to overcome religion and law; the
yoke He gives them is a "new being" above religion. The
thing they will learn from him is the victory over the
law of the wise and the understanding, and the law of
the Scribes and Pharisees.

How does this concern us? Why does this concern all
men, in all situations? It concerns us because, with all
human beings, we are sighing under the law, under a
law which is religion and a religion which is law. This
is the depth of the word of Jesus; this is the truth, implied in the emotional power of His words. Man labors
and toils, because he is that being which knows about
his finitude, about his transitoriness, about the danger
of living, and about the tragic character of existence.
Fear and anxiety are the heritage of all people, as Paul
knew when he looked at the Jews and the Pagans. Restlessness drives man during his whole life, as Augustine
knew. A hidden element of despair is in every man's
soul, as the great Danish Protestant, Kierkegaard, discovered. There is no religious genius, no keen observer
of the abyss of the human soul, nobody capable of listening to the sounds of his heart, who would not witness
to this insight into human nature and human existence.
Splits and gaps are in every soul: for instance, we know
that we are more than dust; and yet we know also that
we are going to be dust. We know that we belong to a
higher order than that of our animal needs and desires;
and yet we know that we shall abuse the higher order
in the service of our lower nature. We know that we are
only small members of the spiritual world; and yet we

know that we shall aspire to the whole, making ourselves the center of the world.

This is man; and because this is man, there is religion and law. The law of religion is the great attempt of man to overcome his anxiety and restlessness and despair, to close the gap within himself, and to reach immortality, spirituality and perfection. So he labors and toils under the religious law in thought and in act.

The religious law demands that he accept ideas and dogmas, that he believe in doctrines and traditions, the acceptance of which is the condition of his salvation from anxiety, despair and death. So he tries to accept them, although they may have become strange or doubtful to him. He labors and toils under the religious demand to believe things he cannot believe. Finally he tries to escape the law of religion. He tries to cast away the heavy yoke of the doctrinal law imposed on him by Church authorities, orthodox teachers, pious parents, and fixed traditions. He becomes critical and sceptical. He casts away the yoke; but none can live in the emptiness of mere scepticism, and so he returns to the old yoke in a kind of self-torturing fanaticism and tries to impose it on other people, on his children or pupils. He is driven by an unconscious desire for revenge, because of the burden he has taken upon himself. Many families are disrupted by painful tragedies and many minds are broken by this attitude of parents, teachers and priests. Others unable to stand the emptiness of scepticism, find new yokes outside the Church, new doctrinal laws under which they begin to labor: political ideologies which they propagate with religious fanaticism; scientific theories which they defend with religious dogmatism; and utopian expectations they pronounce as the condition of salvation for the world, forcing whole nations under the yoke of their creeds which are religions, even while they pretend to destroy religion. We are all laboring under the yoke of religion; we all, sometimes, try to throw away old or new doctrines or dogmas, but after a little while we return, again enslaving ourselves and others in their servitude.

The same is true of the practical laws of religion. They demand ritual activities, the participation in religious enterprises, and the study of religious traditions, prayer, sacraments and meditations. They demand moral obedience, inhuman self-control and asceticism, devotion to man and things beyond our possibilities, surrender to ideas and duties beyond our power, unlimited self-negation, and unlimited self-perfection: the religious law demands the perfect in all respects. And our conscience agrees with this demand. But the split in our being is derived from just this: that the perfect, although it is the truth, is beyond us, against us, judging and condemning us. So we try to throw away the ritual and moral demands. We neglect them, we hate them, we criticize them; some of us display a cynical indifference toward the religious and moral law. But since mere cynicism is as impossible as mere scepticism, we return to old or new laws, becoming more fanatic than ever before, and take a yoke of the law upon us, which is more self-defying, more cruel against ourselves, and more willing to coerce other people under the same yoke in the name of the perfect. Jesus Himself becomes for these perfectionists, puritans and moralists a teacher of the religious law putting upon us the heaviest of all burdens, the burden of *His* law. But that is the greatest possible distortion of the mind of Jesus. This distortion can be found in the minds of those who crucified Him because He broke the religious law, not by fleeing from it like the cynical Sadducees, but by overcoming it. We are all permanently in danger of abusing Jesus by stating that He is the founder of a new religion, and the bringer of another, more refined, and more enslaving law. And so we see in all Christian Churches the toiling and laboring of people who are called Christians, serious Christians, under innumerable laws which they cannot fulfill, from which they flee, to which they return, or which they replace by other laws. This is the yoke from which Jesus wants to liberate us. He is more than a priest or a prophet or a religious genius. These all subject us to religion. He frees us from religion. They all make new religious laws; He overcomes the religious law.

"Take my yoke upon you and learn of me . . . for my yoke is easy and my burden is light." This does not indicate a quantitative difference—a little easier, a little lighter. It indicates a contradiction! The yoke of Jesus is easy in itself, because it is above law, and replaces the toiling and laboring with rest in our souls. The yoke of religion and law presupposes all those splits and gaps in our souls which drive us to the attempt to overcome them. The yoke of Jesus is above those splits and gaps. It has overcome them whenever it appears and is received. It is not a new demand, a new doctrine or new morals, but rather a new reality, a new being and a new power of transforming life. He calls it a yoke, He means that it comes from above and grasps us with saving force; if He calls it easy, He means that it is not a matter of our acting and striving, but rather that it is given before anything we can do. It is being, power, reality, conquering the anxiety and despair, the fear and the restlessness of our existence. It is here, amongst us, in the midst of our personal tragedy, and the tragedy of history. Suddenly, within the hardest struggle, it appears as a victory, not attained by ourselves, but present beyond expectation and struggle. Suddenly we are grasped by a peace which is above reason, that is, above our theoretical seeking for the true, and above our practical striving for the good. The true—namely, the truth of our life and of our existence—has grasped us. We know that *now*, in this moment, we are in the truth, in spite of all our ignorance about ourselves and our world. We have not become wiser and more understanding in any ordinary sense; we are still children in knowledge. But the truth of life is in us, with an illuminating certainty, uniting us with ourselves, giving us great and restful happiness. And the good, the ultimate good, which is not good for something else, but good in itself, has grasped us. We know that now, in this moment, we are in the good, in spite of all our weakness and evil, in spite of the fragmentary and distorted character of our Self and the world. We have not become more moral or more saintly; we still belong to a world which is subject to evil and self-destruction. But the good of life is in us, uniting us with the good of everything, giving us the blessed experience of universal love. If this should happen, and in such a measure, we should reach our eternity, the higher order and spiritual world to which we belong, and from which we are separated in our normal existence. We should be beyond ourselves. The new being would conquer us, although the old being would not disappear.

Where can we feel this new reality? We cannot find it; but it can find us. It tries to find us during our whole life. It is in the world; it carries the world; and it is the cause of the fact that our Self and our world are not yet thrown into utter self-destruction. Although it is hid-

den under anxiety and despair, under finitude and tragedy, it is in everything, in souls and bodies, because
everything derives life from it. The new being means
that the old being has not yet destroyed itself completely; that life is still possible; that our souls still gather
force to go forward; and that the good and the true are
not extinguished. It is present, and it will find us. Let us
be found by it. It is stronger than the world, although
it is quiet and meek and humble.

That is the meaning of the call of Jesus, "Come unto
Me." For in Him this new being is present in such a way
that it determines His life. That which is hidden in all
things, that which appears to us sometimes in the great
elevations of our soul, is the forming power of this life. It
is the uniqueness and the mystery of His Being, the
embodiment, the full appearance of the New Being.
That is the reason that He can say words which no
prophet or saint has ever said: that nobody knows God
save Him and those who receive their knowledge
through Him. These words certainly do not mean that
He imposes a new theology or a new religious law upon
us. They mean rather that He is the New Being in which
everybody can participate, because it is universal and
omnipresent. Why can He call Himself meek and lowly
in heart after he has said words about His uniqueness,
words that, in anyone else's mouth, would be blasphemous arrogance? It is because the New Being that forms
Him is not created by Him. He is created by it. It has
found Him, as it must find us. And since His Being is
not the result of His striving and laboring, and since it
is not servitude to the religious law but rather victory
over religion and law that makes His uniqueness, He
does not impose religion and law, burdens and yokes,
upon men. We would turn down His call with hatred

if He called us to the Christian religion or to the Chris
tian doctrines or to the Christian morals. We would not
accept His claim to be meek and humble and to give
rest to our souls, if He gave us new commands for
thinking and acting. Jesus is not the creator of another
religion, but the victor over religion; He is not the maker
of another law, but the conqueror of law. We, the ministers and teachers of Christianity, do not call you to
Christianity but rather to the New Being to which Christianity should be a witness and nothing else, not con-
fusing itself with that New Being. Forget all Christian
doctrines; forget your own certainties and your own
doubts, when you hear the call of Jesus. Forget all Christian morals, your achievements and your failures, when
you come to Him. Nothing is demanded of you—no idea
of God, and no goodness in yourselves, not your being
religious, not your being Christian, not your being wise,
and not your being moral. But what is demanded is
only your being open and willing to accept what is given
to you, the New Being, the being of love and justice and
truth, as it is manifest in Him Whose yoke is easy and
Whose burden is light.

Let me close, as I began, with a personal word. Believe me, you who are religious and Christian. It would
not be worthwhile to teach Christianity, if it were for
the sake of Christianity. And believe me, you who are
estranged from religion and far away from Christianity,
it is not our purpose to make you religious and Christian when we interpret the call of Jesus for our time. We
call Jesus the Christ not because He brought a new religion, but because He is the end of religion, above religion and irreligion, above Christianity and non-Chris-
tianity. We spread His call because it is the call to every
man in every period to receive the New Being, that hid-

den saving power in our existence, which takes from us labor and burden, and gives rest to our souls.

Do not ask in this moment what we shall do or how action shall follow from the New Being, from the rest in our souls. Do not ask; for you do not ask how the good fruits follow from the goodness of a tree. They follow; action follows being, and new action, better action, stronger action, follows new being, better being, stronger being. We and our world would be better, truer, and more just, if there were more rest for souls in our world. Our actions would be more creative, more conquering, conquering the tragedy of our time, if they grew out of a more profound level of our life. For our creative depth is the depth in which we are quiet.

12

THE MEANING OF PROVIDENCE

For I am persuaded, that neither death, nor life, nor angels, nor principalities, nor powers, nor things present, nor things to come, nor height, nor depth, nor any other creature, shall be able to separate us from the love of God, which is in Christ Jesus our Lord.   ROMANS 8:38-39.

THESE WELL-KNOWN WORDS OF PAUL express the Christian faith in divine Providence. They are the first and fundamental interpretation of the disturbing words in the gospel of Matthew, where Jesus commands us not to take any thought about our life and food and clothing, and to seek first the Kingdom of God, for all of our daily life and needs are already known by God. We need such an interpretation. For there are few articles of the Christian faith which are more important for the daily life of every man and woman, and there are few more open to misunderstanding and distortion. And such misunderstanding necessarily leads to a disillusionment which not only turns the hearts of men away from God, but also creates a revolt against Him, against Christianity, and against religion. When I spoke to the soldiers between the battles of the last war, they expressed their denial of the Christian message in terms of an attack upon the belief in Providence—an

attack which obviously drew its bitterness from fundamental disappointments. After reading a paper written
by the great Einstein, in which he challenges the faith
in a personal God, I concluded that there was no difference between his feeling and that of the unsophisticated
soldiers. The idea of God seemed to be impossible, because the reality of our world seems to be in opposition
to the all-mighty power of a wise and righteous God.

Once, when I tried to interpret to a group of Christian and Jewish refugees the paradoxical character of
the divine world-government in terms of Second Isaiah,
a formerly eminent Jew from Western Germany told me
that he had received many cablegrams from Southern
France informing him of the horrible story of the sudden evacuation, from Germany, of nearly ten thousand
Jews, of the age of ninety or more, and of their trans-
portation to the concentration camps. He said that the
thought of this unimaginable misery prevented him from
being able to find meaning in even the most powerful
message concerning the divine Providence. What answer
shall we give, what answer *can* we give to such a crucial
problem—a problem in which Christianity as a whole
is at stake, a problem which has nothing to do with a
theoretical criticism of the idea of God, but rather which
represents the anguish of the human heart which can
no longer stand the power borne by the daemonic
forces on earth?

Paul speaks of these forces. He knows them all: the
horror of death and the anxiety of life; the irresistible
strength of natural and historic powers; the ambiguity
of the present and the inscrutable darkness of the future;
the incalculable turns of fate from height to depth, and
from depth to height; and the natural destruction of
creature by creature. He knows them all as well as we

do, who have, in our period, rediscovered them, after a short time in which Providence and reality seemed to be a matter of fact. But it never was, and never will be, a matter of fact. It is rather a matter of the most powerful, the most paradoxical, and the most venturing faith. Only as such has it meaning and truth.

What is its content? It is certainly not a vague promise that, with the help of God, everything will come to a good end; there are many things that come to a bad end. And it is not the maintenance of hope in every situation; there are situations in which there can be no hope. Nor is it the anticipation of a period of history, in which divine Providence will be proved by human happiness and goodness; there is no generation in which divine Providence will be less paradoxical than it is in ours. But the content of the faith in Providence is this: when death rains from heaven as it does now, when cruelty wields power over nations and individuals as it does now, when hunger and persecution drive millions from place to place as they do now, and when prisons and slums all over the world distort the humanity of the bodies and souls of men as they do now—we can boast in that time, and just in that time, that even all of this cannot separate us from the love of God. In this sense, and in this sense alone, all things work together for good, for the *ultimate* good, the eternal love, and the Kingdom of God. Faith in divine Providence is the faith that nothing can prevent us from fulfilling the ultimate meaning of our existence. Providence does not mean a divine planning by which everything is predetermined, as is an efficient machine. Rather, Providence means that there is a creative and saving possibility implied in every situation, which cannot be destroyed by any event. Providence means that the daemonic and destructive forces within ourselves and our world can never have an unbreakable grasp upon us, and that the bond which connects us with the fulfilling love can never be disrupted.

This love appears to us and is embodied in "Christ Jesus our Lord". By adding this, Paul does not use a merely solemn phrase, as we often do when we use the words. He uses them, rather, after he has pointed to the only thing that can destroy our faith in Providence, which is our disbelief in the love of God, our distrust of God, our fear of His wrath, our hatred of his Presence, our conception of Him as a tyrant who condemns us, and our feeling of sin and guilt. It is not the depth of our suffering, but the depth of our separation from God, which destroys our faith in Providence. Providence and the forgiveness of sins are not two separate aspects of the Christian faith; they are one and the same—the certainty that we can reach eternal life in spite of suffering and sin. Paul unites both words by saying, "Who is he that condemneth? It is Christ Jesus . . . who maketh intercession for us", and *therefore,* he continues, "Who shall separate us from the love of Christ? Shall tribulation, or anguish, or persecution, or famine, or nakedness, or peril, or sword . . . ? In all these things we are more than conquerors through him who loved us. . . ." *This* is the faith in Providence, and this alone.

13

KNOWLEDGE THROUGH LOVE

*Love never faileth; but whether there be prophe-
cies, they shall fail; whether there be tongues, they
shall cease; whether there be knowledge, it shall
vanish away. For we know in part, and we prophesy
in part. But when that which is perfect is come, then
that which is in part shall be done away. When I was
a child, I spake as a child, I understood as a child,
I thought as a child: but when I became a man, I put
away childish things. For now we see through a
glass, darkly; but then face to face: now I know in
part; but then shall I know even as also I am known.*
                                    I CORINTHIANS 13:8-12.

PAUL SPEAKS, IN THE FAMOUS WORDS
of our text, of things which are in part—or, as we should
say today, fragmentary things—and of the things which
are perfect, or complete. The fragmentary things shall
vanish away; the complete things shall abide. The former are temporal; the latter are eternal. The fragmentary, temporal things are not merely material; they are
some of the highest gifts of the Divine Spirit: prophecy,
which is the interpretation of our time and history;
tongues, which are our ecstatic feeling and speaking; and
knowledge, which is the understanding of our existence.

Even those spiritual goods shall disappear with all the material and intellectual goods. They are all fragmentary, temporal, transitory. Love alone does not disappear; it endures forever. For God Himself is love, according to John who carries through the thought of Paul.

But there is another consideration in our text which seems to contradict the words about love. Paul singles out knowledge, and points to the difference between our fragmentary, indirect and darkened knowledge, and the full, direct and total knowledge to come. He compares the childish imaginations with the mature insights of the adult. He speaks of something which, besides love, is perfect and eternal—namely, the seeing of the truth, face to face; the knowledge which is as full as God's knowledge of us.

How are these two considerations united? Did Paul forget that he had just predicted the perfection and eternity of love alone? No, he did not forget; for he closes this part of his letter by re-emphasizing the abiding character of love as the greatest thing of all. Or are the words about knowledge inserted without thought of a definite connection with the rest of the passage? They are not merely inserted; for there is a link, one of the most profound phrases in this great chapter: ". . . even as also *I* am fully known"— fully known, that is, by God. But there is only one way to know a personality—to become united with that personality through love. Full knowledge presupposes full love. God knows me, because He loves me; and I shall know Him face to face through a similar uniting, which is love and knowledge at the same time. Love lasts; love alone endures, and nothing else besides love, nothing independent of love. Yet, in love, the seeing face to face and the knowledge of the centre of the other *I* are implied. It is not blind love that is the enduring love, the love that God Himself *is*. It is a seeing love, a knowing love, a love that looks through into the depth of the Heart of God, and into the depth of our hearts. There is no strangeness to love; love knows; it is the only power of complete and lasting knowledge. There is a Greek word which can designate both knowledge and sensual love. It can designate both, because both meanings express an act of union, an over-coming of the cleavage between beings. Knowledge shall be done away with in so far as it is different from love; knowledge shall become eternal in so far as it is one with love. Therefore, the standard of knowledge is the standard of love. For Paul, the difference between knowledge and love, between seeing and acting, be-tween theory and practice, exists only when fragmentary knowledge is our concern. Full knowledge does not ad-mit a difference between itself and love, or between theory and practice. Love overcomes the seeming oppo-sition between theory and practice; it is knowing and doing at the same time. Therefore, it is the greatest thing of all; therefore, God Himself is love; therefore, the Christ, as the manifestation of the Divine Love, is full of grace *and* of truth. That is what Paul means; and that is the standard of knowledge he gives.

And now let us consider our existence, and the knowl-edge that we possess. Paul says that all our present knowledge is like the preception of things in a mirror, that it therefore concerns enigmas and riddles. This is only another way of expressing the fragmentary charac-ter of our knowledge. For fragments out of the context of the whole are only riddles to us. We may surmise the nature of the whole; we may approach the whole indi-rectly; but we do not see the whole itself; we do not grasp it directly face to face. A little light and much darkness; a few fragments and never the whole; many problems and never a solution; only reflections in the mirrors of our souls, without the source of truth itself: that is the situation of our knowledge. And it is the situation of our love. Because the love which is perfect and lasting lies not within us, perfect knowledge is denied us. Since, as beings, we are separated from each other, and therefore from this ultimate unity, the community of knowledge among single beings is made impossible, as it is also, then, between beings and the Ground of Being Itself. A great philosopher has said that our knowledge reaches as far as our creative will reaches. That is true for a certain realm of life. But it is not true for the whole of our life. The fact that our knowledge reaches as far as our uniting love reaches is valid for the whole of human existence.

Mankind has always tried to decipher the puzzling fragments of life. That attempt is not just a matter for the philosophers or priests or prophets or wise men in all periods of history. It is a matter for everyone. For every man is a fragment himself. He is a riddle to himself; and the individual life of everyone else is an enigma to him, dark, puzzling, embarrassing, exciting, and torturing. Our very being is a continuous asking for the *meaning* of our being, a continuous attempt to decipher the enigma of our world and our heart. Before children are adjusted to the conventional reactions of adults and have grown out of their creative individuality, they show the continuous asking, the urgent desire to decipher the riddles they see in the primitive mirror of their experience. The creative man, in all realms of life, is like a child, who dares to inquire beyond the limits of conventional answers. He discovers the fragmentary character of all these answers, a character darkly and subconsciously felt by all men. He may destroy, by means of one fundamental question, a whole, well-organized system of life and society, of ethics and religion. He may show that what people believed to be a whole is nothing but a fragment of a fragment. He may shake the certainty on which centuries lived, by unearthing a riddle or an enigma in its very foundation. The misery of man lies in the fragmentary character of his life and knowledge; the greatness of man lies in his ability to know that his being is fragmentary and enigmatic. For man is able to be puzzled and to ask, to go beyond the fragments, seeking the perfect. Yet, in being able to do so, he feels at the same time the tragedy implicit in his being, the tragedy of the riddle and the fragment. Man is subject, with all beings, to the law of vanity. But man alone is conscious of that law. He is therefore infinitely more miserable than all other beings in the servitude to that law; on the other hand, he is infinitely superior, because he alone knows that there is something beyond vanity and decay, beyond riddles and enigmas. This is felt by Paul, when he says that the creation itself shall be delivered from the bondage of decay into the liberty of the glory of the children of God.

Man is a fragment and a riddle to himself. The more he experiences and knows that fact, the more he is really man. Paul experienced the breakdown of a system of life and thought which he believed to be a whole, a perfect truth without riddle or gaps. He then found himself buried under the pieces of his knowledge and his morals. But Paul never tried again to build up a new, comfortable house out of the pieces. He dwelt with the pieces. He realized always that fragments remain fragments, even if one attempts to reorganize them. The unity to which they belong lies beyond them; it is grasped through hope, but not face to face.

How could Paul endure life, as it lay in fragments? He endured it because the fragments bore a new meaning to him. The pictures in the mirror pointed to something new for him: they anticipated the perfect, the reality of love. Through the pieces of his knowledge and morality, love appeared to him. And the power of love transformed the tormenting riddles into symbols of truth, the tragic fragments into symbols of the whole.

14

DOING THE TRUTH

For God sent not his Son into the world to condemn the world; but that the world through him might be saved. He that believeth on him is not condemned: but he that believeth not is condemned already, because he hath not believed in the name of the only begotten Son of God. And this is the condemnation, that light is come into the world, and men loved darkness rather than light, because their deeds were evil. For everyone that doeth evil hateth the light, neither cometh to the light, lest his deeds should be reproved. But he that doeth truth cometh to the light, that his deeds may be made manifest, that they are wrought in God. JOHN 3:17-21.

HE THAT DOES THE TRUTH! THIS IS A VERY surprising combination of words. We may recognize and know the truth, and we may act sometimes according to our knowledge, but how can we *do* the truth? The truth is given to us in a true theory. We may or we may not follow that theory in our practice. Theory and practice seem to be two different things, and it is difficult to think of them united. Similarly, it is difficult to understand the phrase "doeth the truth". Perhaps this phrase should not be taken too seriously. Perhaps it should

114

simply be interpreted as "acting according to the truth". But if such an interpretation were correct, what about the statements, also to be found in the Fourth Gospel, "I am the truth", "the truth has become", and that which speaks of people "who are of the truth"? None of these statements would have meaning if truth were a matter of theory alone.

People sometimes say, "This is right in theory but it doesn't work in practice." They ought to say, "This is wrong in theory and consequently it is wrong in practice." There is no true theory which could be wrong in practice. This contrast between theory and practice is contrived by people who want to escape hard and thorough thinking. They like to abide in the shallowness of accustomed practices, on the surface of a so-called "experience". They will accept nothing but a repeated confirmation of something they already know or believe. Only those questions for truth which have challenged and disturbed centuries of practice have brought about a fundamental transformation of practice. This is true of the history of science, morals and religion. When the prophet Amos questioned the theory of all pagan religions, that the being and power of God is in some way identified with the being and power of a special country, the pagan practice all over the world was undermined. When the prophet of the exile questioned the theory that the suffering of a nation is the punishment for its own sins, and explored the theory that the suffering of the servant of God serves all nations, the history of mankind received a new character. When the Apostles questioned the theory that the Messiah is an earthy ruler, and explained the Cross of Christ in terms of salvation, the whole system of ancient values was shaken. When Augustine challenged the theory that

God and man work together for salvation; when Luther attacked the theory that there is no salvation without the sacramental mediation of the Church; and when modern historical science destroyed the mechanistic and superstitious doctrines of inspiration, the practice of large sections of mankind was changed. The emphasis laid on truth in the Fourth Gospel should prevent us from being taken in by the misleading contrast between theory and practice. And it should give an urgent impetus toward more thorough thinking to those who are especially concerned with the truth of Christianity.

The Greek word for truth means: making manifest the hidden. Truth is hidden and must be discovered. No one possesses it naturally. It dwells in the depth, beneath the surface. The surface of our existence changes, moving continually like the waves in the ocean, and it is therefore delusive. The depth is eternal and therefore certain. In using the Greek word, the Fourth Gospel accepts the Greek concept, but at the same time it transforms it. "Doing the truth", "being of the truth", "the truth has become", "I am the truth"—all these combinations of words indicate that truth in Christianity is something which *happens*, something which is bound to a special place, to a special time, to a special personality. Truth is something new, something which is *done* by God in history, and, because of this, something which is *done* in the individual life. Truth is hidden, truth is mystery—in Christianity as well as in Greek thought. But the mystery of truth in Christianity is an event which has taken place and which takes place again and again It is life, personal life, revelation and decision. Truth is a stream of life, centered in Christ, actualized in everybody who is connected with Him, organized in the assembly of God, the Church. In Greek thought truth only can be found. In Christianity truth is found if it is done, and done if it is found. In Greek thought truth is the manifestation of the eternal, immovable essence of things. In Christianity truth is the new creation, realizing itself in history. Therefore, in Christianity the opposite of truth is lie, and not—as it was in Greece—opinion. The decision for or against truth is *the* life-and-death decision, and this decision is identical with the decision in which Christ is accepted or rejected. You cannot have *opinion* about the Christ after you have faced Him. You can only do the truth by following Him, or do the lie by denying Him. Therefore, it is impossible to make Him a teacher of truth among—or even above—other teachers of truth. This would separate the truth from Him, and the decision for truth from the decision for Him (just as the decision for Plato's teaching is not the same thing as the decision for Plato). But just this separation is denied by the Fourth Gospel, when it calls Christ the truth "which has become", and when it calls his followers those who are of the truth, and who, therefore, are able to do the truth.

Christian theology is rooted in the concept of truth in which no cleavage between theory and practice is admitted, because this truth is saving truth. Theology should be like a circle in which the most peripheral elements of the historical, educational, and philosophical theories are directed toward the center, the truth, which is the Christ. No statement is theological which does not contain, directly or indirectly, saving truth. And "saving truth" means that truth which is done; saving truth is in "him that does the truth."

15

THE THEOLOGIAN* (Part I)

Now concerning spiritual gifts, brethren, I would not have you ignorant. Ye know that ye were Gentiles, carried away unto these dumb idols, even as ye were led. Wherefore I give you to understand, that no man speaking by the Spirit of God calleth Jesus accursed: and that no man can say that Jesus is the Lord, but by the Holy Ghost. Now there are diversities of gifts, but the same Spirit. And there are differences of administrations, but the same Lord. And there are diversities of operations, but it is the same God which worketh all in all. But the manifestation of the Spirit is given to every man to profit withal. For to one is given by the Spirit the word of wisdom; to another the word of knowledge by the same Spirit; to another faith by the same Spirit; to another the gifts of healing by the same Spirit; to another the working of miracles; to another prophecy; to another discerning of spirits; to another divers kinds of tongues; to another the interpretation of tongues: but all these worketh that one and the selfsame Spirit, dividing to every man severally as he will. I CORINTHIANS 12:1-11.

* This sermon, and the two succeeding sermons were given with students of theology especially in mind.

MOST OF US ARE STUDENTS OF THEOLOGY, whether we teach or learn, whether we be missionaries or educators, ministers or social workers, administrators or political leaders. But in this particular community, we are *theologians*, persons who ask the question of our ultimate concern, the question of God and His manifestation. Whatever else we may be, we are first of all theologians. Therefore, it is most natural—although not most usual—for us to consider our existence as theologians. On what is this existence based? What makes a man a theologian? What is his relation to other forms of existence? What is the significance of our existence as a whole? Paul makes very clear what he thinks is the foundation of all theology: the Divine Spirit. And the word of wisdom and knowledge, theology, according to the witness of the whole Christian Church, is basically a gift of the Spirit. It is *one* of the gifts, besides others. It is a *special* gift, besides other special gifts. But it is a *gift* of the Spirit, and not a natural capacity. The word of knowledge—theology—is spoken *to us* before *we* can say it to others, or even to ourselves. To be a theologian means first of all to be able to *receive* spiritual knowledge. But on the basis of this criterion, can we call ourselves theologians? Can we say that *our* theological thought is a gift of the Spirit? Are we certain that our theological existence transcends our human capacities, or that we have the word of knowledge, the word of spiritual wisdom?

Paul gives a very concrete criterion for theological existence, which is also the criterion for all spiritual existence. He says: He who cries "Cursed be Jesus" does not speak in the Spirit of God; and no one can say "Jesus is Lord" except in the Holy Spirit. He who accepts Jesus as the Christ proves by that very acceptance

that he has received the Spirit of God. For the spirit of
man alone is not capable of making the statement: "I
accept Jesus as the Christ". That statement is the mystery
and the foundation of the Christian Church, the paradox and the stumbling-block, which produce curses
against Christianity. It is the depth and the power which
create a new Being in the world, in history, and in
man. Therefore, he who joins in the Church's confession that Jesus is the Christ participates in the Divine
Spirit. It is he who *can* receive the Spirit of wisdom and
knowledge; it is he who *can* become a theologian.

Theology does not exist outside the community of
those who affirm that Jesus is the Christ, outside the
Church, the assembly of God. Theology is a work of
the Church, precisely because it is a gift of the Divine
Spirit. Theological existence is an element of the existence of the Church. It is not simply a matter of "free"
thinking, of scientific research, or of general philosophical analysis. Theology expresses the faith of the Church.
It restates the paradoxical statement, *Jesus is the Christ,*
and considers all its presuppositions and implications.
Theological existence indicates the existence of one who
is grasped, within the Church, by the Divine Spirit, and
who has received the word of wisdom and knowledge.

But we must ask another question. If that be theological existence, which one of us can call himself a
theologian? Who can decide to become a theologian?
And who can dare to remain a theologian? Do we really
belong to the assembly of God? Can we seriously accept
the paradox upon which the Church is built, the paradox that Jesus is the Christ? Are we grasped by the
Divine Spirit, and have we received the word of knowledge as a gift? If somebody were to come and tell us
that he *certainly* belongs to the Church, that he does

not doubt that Jesus is the Christ any longer, that he continuously experiences the grip of the Divine Spirit and the gift of spiritual knowledge, what should be our answer to him? We certainly should tell him that he does not fulfill even the first condition of theological existence, which is the realization that one does *not* know whether he has experienced the Divine Spirit, or spirits which are not divine. We would not accept him as a theologian. On the other hand, if someone were to come and tell us that he is estranged from the Christian Church and its foundations, that he does not feel the presence of the power of the Spirit, that he is empty of spiritual knowledge, *but* that he asks again and again the theological question, the question of an ultimate concern and its manifestations in Jesus as the Christ, we would accept him as a theologian. Perhaps we would test the seriousness of his doubt, in order to see whether his emptiness and despair expressed a new and more refined vanity. But if we were convinced of his seriousness, we would consider him a theologian.

There are many amongst us who believe within themselves that they can never become good theologians, that they could do better in almost any other realm. Yet they cannot imagine that their existence could be anything other than theological existence. Even if they had to give up theology as their vocational work, they would never cease to ask the theological question. It would pursue them into every realm. They would be bound to it, actually, if not vocationally. They could not be sure that they could fulfill its demands, but they would be sure that they were in its bondage. They who believe those things in their hearts belong to the assembly of God. They are grasped by the Divine Spirit. They have received the gift of knowledge. They are theologians.

THE THEOLOGIAN (Part II)

For though I be free from all men, yet have I made myself servant unto all, that I might gain the more. And unto the Jews I became as a Jew, that I might gain the Jews; to them that are under the law, as under the law, that I might gain them that are under the law; to them that are without law, as without law (being not without law to God, but under the law to Christ), that I might gain them that are without law. To the weak became I as weak, that I might gain the weak: I am made all things to all men, that I might by all means save some. And this I do for the gospel's sake, that I might be partaker thereof with you. I CORINTHIANS 9:19-23.

WE HAVE SEEN IN THE FIRST SERMON that the foundation of our theological existence is that the Divine Spirit keeps us in its power, and makes it impossible for us ever to escape the theological question, the question of our ultimate concern, the question of God. We considered the theologian as a believer in spite of his doubt and despair, and as a member of the Church, in whose power all theological work is done, in spite of his lack of certainty.

Now, some words of Paul about his ministry shall lead us to the understanding of another side of our theological existence. An apostle is certainly more than a theologian; and a minister exercises more functions than a theological scholar. But an apostle is *also* a theologian; and a minister cannot work without theology. Therefore, the words that Paul says about his ministry as a whole are *also* true of the theological part of his ministry: "To all men I have become all things." Theological existence demands the same attitude. The theologian, *in his theology,* must become all things to all men. We must consider the meaning of those words.

"To those under the Law I have become as one of themselves, to win those under the Law, although I am not under the Law myself." Let us replace the word "Law" by "idealism", not only because idealists are usually legalistic, but also because idealism is a noble attitude, which elevates us above the lower strata of our existence, and produces faith and devotion, just as the Law does. "To the idealists I have become as one of themselves, to win those who are idealists, although I am not an idealist myself." How is such an act possible? How can the theologian, not being an idealist, become an idealist to the idealists? He can become an idealist in exactly the same way as the apostle of Christ can become a Jew to the Jews. Paul says that the Law is good, and that it is not abolished, but rather fulfilled, in Christ. Likewise, the theologian who is not an idealist (and who could never be an idealist) does not destroy idealism. He utilizes it and states that it contains some truth which creates a continuous temptation for the theologian to become an idealist himself, and to deny the Cross which is the judgment over idealism. The theologian uses idealism, its concepts and methods. He becomes a Platonist to the Platonists, a Stoic to the Stoics, an Hegelian to the Hegelians, a progressivist to the progressivists. But he cannot confuse any of these

forms of idealism with the Christian message. He ad-
heres more to some than to others. But he never imposes
his preferred form upon others in the name of Christianity. He is aware of the despair that idealism, as well
as the Law, can bring upon us. And he knows that in
Christ there is a new Being in which all ideals are embodied and have become visible, no longer as ideals, but
as realities.

"To those outside the Law I have become as one of
them (although I am under Christ's law, and not outside God's Law), in order to triumph over those outside
the Law." Let us replace the phrase "outside the Law"
by "realism", not because the realists have no Law (for
neither they nor the pagans are without some Law),
but because they have no abstract principles to impose
upon reality. Their greatness lies in their humble acceptance of things as they are. "The piety of realism is
humility." "To the realists I have become as one of
themselves, in order to win them, although I am not a
realist myself." The theologian who is not a realist (and
who could never become a realist) does not destroy
realism. He recognizes the truth of realism, and is continually tempted to become a realist himself, and thus
to deny the eternal life which is the judgment over realism. The theologian uses realism and becomes a posi-
tivist to the positivists, a pragmatist to the pragmatists,
and a tragic interpreter of life to the tragic interpreters
of life. But he does not say that realism is the Christian
message. He does not fight for it in the name of Christianity He knows the despair of mere realism, and he
knows that there is a new Being which overcomes the
self-destruction of reality.

"To the weak I have become weak myself in order to
gain the weak." This is the most profound of the three

statements that Paul makes about himself, and the most important one for our existence as theologians. We must become *as though weak*, although, grasped by the Divine Spirit, the basis of all theology, we are not weak. How can we become weak without being already weak? We can become weak by having the strength to acknowledge our weakness, by restraining ourselves from all fanaticism and theological self-certainty, and by participating—not from the outside, but from the inside—in the weakness of all those to whom we speak as theologians. Our strength is *our weakness*; our strength is not *our* strength. We are strong, therefore, only in so far as we point, for our own sake and for the sake of others, to the truth which possesses us, but which we do not possess.

Nothing is more disastrous for the theologian himself and more despicable to those whom he wants to convince than a theology of self-certainty. The real theologian is he who has the strength to perceive and to confess his weakness, and who, therefore, has the strength to become *as weak to the weak*, so that his is the victory.

THE THEOLOGIAN (Part III)

Then Paul stood in the midst of Mars' hill, and said, Ye men of Athens, I perceive that in all things ye are too superstitious. For as I passed by, and beheld your devotions, I found an altar with this inscription, TO THE UNKNOWN GOD. Whom therefore ye ignorantly worship, him declare I unto you. God that made the world and all things therein, seeing that he is Lord of heaven and earth, dwelleth not in temples made with hands; neither is worshipped with men's hands, as though he needed anything, seeing he giveth to all life, and breath, and all things; and hath made of one blood all nations of men for to dwell on all the face of the earth, and hath determined the times before appointed, and the bounds of their habitation; that they should seek the Lord, if haply they might feel after him, and find him, though he be not far from every one of us: for in him we live, and move, and have our being; as certain also of your own poets have said, For we are also his offspring. Forasmuch then as we are the offspring of God, we ought not to think that the Godhead is like unto gold, or silver, or stone, graven by art and man's device. And the times of this ignorance God winked at; but now commandeth all men everywhere to repent: because he hath appointed a day, in the which he will judge the world in righteousness by that man whom he hath ordained; whereof he hath given assurance unto all men, in that he hath raised him from the dead. And when they heard of the resurrection of the dead, some mocked; and others said, We will hear thee again of this matter.

ACTS 17:22-32.

THE FIRST TIME I SPOKE OF OUR EXISTENCE as theologians, I indicated that the foundation of this existence lay in the power of the Divine Spirit and in the reality of the Church. It was the *believing* theolo-

gian—believing in spite of all his doubts and despairs—
that I tried to describe. The second time that we considered our existence as theologians, we looked at the
self-surrendering theologian who, through the power of
love, becomes "all things to all men", that theologian
who seems to lose himself through the understanding of
everything and everyone. This time let us think about
the *answering* theologian who, in spite of his participation in the weakness and error of all men, is able to
answer their questions through the power of his foundation, the New Being in Christ.

The famous scene in which Paul speaks from the central place of Greek wisdom shows us a man who is the
prototype of the *answering* theologian. Paul has been
asked about his message, partly because the Athenians
were always curious about novelties, and partly because
they knew that they did *not* know the truth, and seriously desired to know it. There are three stages in Paul's
answer, which reveal the three tasks of the *answering*
theologian. The first stage of Paul's answer consists in
the assertion that those who ask him the ultimate question are not unconscious of the answer: these men adore
an unknown God and thus witness to their religious
knowledge in spite of their religious ignorance. That
knowledge is not astounding, because God is close to
each one of us; it is in *Him* that we live and move and
exist; these *also* belong to His race. The first answer,
then, that we must give to those who ask us about such
a question is that they themselves are already aware of
the answer. We must show to them that neither they
nor we are outside of God, that even the atheists stand
in God—namely, that power out of which they live, the
truth for which they grope, and the ultimate meaning of
life in which they believe. It is bad theology and religious

cowardice ever to think that there may be a place where
we could look *at* God, as though He were something
outside of us to be argued for or against. Genuine atheism is not humanly possible, for God is nearer to a man
than that man is to himself. A God can only be denied
in the name of another God; and God appearing in *one*
form can be denied only by God appearing in another
form. That is the first answer that we must give to ourselves and to those who question us, not as an abstract
statement, but rather as a continuous interpretation of
our human existence, in all its hidden motions and
abysses and certainties.

God is nearer to us than we ourselves. We cannot find
a place outside of Him; but we can *try* to find such a
place. The second part of Paul's answer is that we can
be in the condition of continuous flight from God. We
can imagine one way of escape after another; we can
replace God by the products of our imagination; and we
do. Although mankind is not strange to God, it is estranged from Him. Although mankind is never without
God, it perverts the picture of God. Although mankind
is never without the knowledge of God, it is ignorant
of God. Mankind is separated from its origin; it lives
under a law of wrath and frustration, of tragedy and
self-destruction, because it produces one distorted image
of God after another, and adores those images. The
answering theologian must discover the false gods in
the individual soul and in society. He must probe into
their most secret hiding-places. He must challenge them
through the power of the Divine Logos, which makes
him a theologian. Theological polemic is not merely a
theoretical discussion, but rather a spiritual judgement
against the gods which are not God, against those structures of evil, those distortions of God in thought and

action. No compromise or adaptation or theological self-surrender is permitted on this level. For the first Commandment is the rock upon which theology stands. There is no synthesis possible between God and the idols. In spite of the dangers inherent in so judging, the theologian must become an instrument of the Divine Judgement against a distorted world.

So far as they can grasp it in the light of their own questions, Paul's listeners are willing to accept this two-fold answer. But Paul then speaks of a third thing which they are not able to bear. They either reject it immediately, or they postpone the decision to reject or accept it. He speaks of a Man Whom God has destined to be the Judgement and the Life of the world. That is the third and final part of the theological answer. For we are real theologians when we state that Jesus is the Christ, and that it is in Him that the Logos of theology is manifest.

But we are only theologians when we interpret this paradox, this stumbling-block for idealism and realism, for the weak and the strong, for both pagans and Jews. As theologians, we must interpret that paradox, and not throw paradoxical phrases at the minds of the people. We must not preserve or produce artificial stumbling-blocks, miracle-stories, legends, myths, and other sophisticated paradoxical talk. We must not distort, by ecclesiastical and theological arrogance, that great cosmic paradox that there is victory over death within the world of death itself. We must not impose the heavy burden of wrong stumbling-blocks upon those who ask us questions. But neither must we empty the true paradox of its power. For true theological existence is the witnessing to Him Whose yoke is easy and Whose burden is light, to Him Who is the true paradox.

16

THE WITNESS OF THE SPIRIT TO THE SPIRIT

There is therefore now no condemnation to them which are in Christ Jesus, who walk not after the flesh, but after the Spirit. For the law of the Spirit of life in Christ Jesus hath made me free from the law of sin and death. For what the law could not do, in that it was weak through the flesh, God sending his own Son in the likeness of sinful flesh, and for sin, condemned sin in the flesh: that the righteousness of the law might be fulfilled in us, who walk not after the flesh, but after the Spirit. For they that are after the flesh do mind the things of the flesh; but they that are after the Spirit, the things of the Spirit. For to be carnally minded is death; but to be spiritually minded is life and peace. Because the carnal mind is enmity against God: for it is not subject to the law of God, neither indeed can be. So then they that are in the flesh cannot please God. But ye are not in the flesh, but in the Spirit, if so be that the Spirit of God dwell in you. Now if any man have not the Spirit of Christ, he is none of his. And if Christ be in you, the body is dead because of sin; but the Spirit is life because of righteousness. But if the Spirit of him that raised up Jesus from the dead dwell in you, he that raised up Christ from the dead shall also quicken

*your mortal bodies by his Spirit that dwelleth in you.
Therefore, brethren, we are debtors, not to the flesh,
to live after the flesh. For if ye live after the flesh, ye
shall die: but if ye through the Spirit do mortify the
deeds of the body, ye shall live. For as many as are
led by the Spirit of God, they are the sons of God.
For ye have not received the spirit of bondage again
to fear; but ye have received the spirit of adoption,
whereby we say, Abba, Father. The Spirit itself
beareth witness with our spirit, that we are the children of God. . . . Likewise the Spirit also helpeth
our infirmities: for we know not what we should
pray for as we ought: but the Spirit itself maketh
intercession for us with groanings which cannot be
uttered. And he that searcheth the hearts knoweth
what is in the mind of the spirit, because he maketh
intercession for the saints according to the will of
God.* ROMANS 8:1-16, 26-27.

THIS SOUNDS DIFFICULT TO OUR MODERN
ears, strange and almost unintelligible. Words like
"spirit" and "flesh," "sin" and "law," "life" and "death," in
their various combinations, appear to us as philosophical
abstractions, rather than as concrete descriptions of
Christian experience. For Paul, however, they express the
most real and the most concrete experience of his life.
This eighth chapter of his letter to the Christians in
Rome is like a hymn praising, in ecstatic words, the
new reality which has appeared to him, which was revealed in history and had transformed his whole exist-

ence. Paul calls this new being "Christ", in so far as it has first become visible in Jesus the Christ. And he calls it "Spirit", in so far as it is a reality in the spirit of every Christian, and in the spirit which constitutes the assembly of Christians in every place and time. Both names designate the same reality. Christ is the Spirit, and the Spirit is the Spirit of Christ. A Christian is one who participates in this new reality, that is, one who has the Spirit. "If any man have not the Spirit of Christ, he is none of his." To be a Christian means to have the Spirit, and any description of Christianity must be a description of the manifestations of the Spirit. Let us follow the description that Paul gives us of the Spirit; and let us compare our own experience with it. In so doing we may discover both how far away we are from the experience of Paul, and, at the same time, how similar our experience is to his. These strange words of his may reveal more to us about our lives than anything our contemporaries may think and write about the nature of man, his life and his destiny.

"The Spirit Himself beareth witness with our spirit that we are the children of God." These words imply that our spirit is unable to give us such assurance. Our spirit, that is, our natural mind, our thought, our will, our emotions, the whole of our interior life, cannot give us the certainty that we are the children of God. This does not mean that Paul depreciates human nature and spirit. On the contrary, in speaking of our spirit, he acknowledges the creativity of man, his similarity to God Who is Spirit, his ability to be free himself, and to liberate all nature, from vanity and the bondage of corruption by his own liberation. "For we are also his offspring," he told the Athenians in his famous speech on the Areopagus, thus confirming their own philosophers. Paul thinks as highly of man as any modern could do. A famous Renaissance philosopher describes, in lyrical words, the position of man at the center of nature, his infinity and creativity, the unity and fulfillment in him of all natural powers. Paul would agree. But Paul knew something more than the Greek philosophers knew, something which the Renaissance philosophers had forgotten, namely, that human spirit is bound to human flesh, and that human flesh is hostile to God.

"Human flesh" does not mean human body. Man's body, according to Paul, can become a temple of the Spirit. But "human flesh" means the natural human inclinations, man's desires, his needs, his way of thinking, the aim of his will, the character of his feeling, in so far as it is separated from the Spirit and is hostile to it. "Flesh" is the distortion of human nature, the abuse of its creativity—the abuse, first of all, of its infinity, in the service of its unlimited desire and its unlimited will to power. This desire, of which we know something through recent psychology, and this will to power, of which we have learned much from modern sociology, are rooted in our individual existence in time and space, in body and flesh. This is what Paul calls the power of distorted flesh.

He describes the will of flesh with a profundity which cannot be equalled. "The carnal mind (mind of the flesh) is enmity against God; for it is not subject to the law of God, *neither indeed can be!*" If we receive a law which we must acknowledge and which, on the other hand, we cannot fulfill, our soul inevitably develops hatred against him who has given the law. The father, being the representative of the law which stands against the child's desire, necessarily becomes the object of the child's unconscious hate, which may become conscious and may appear with tremendous force. This would not be so if the law against its unordered and unrestricted desire were felt by the child to be arbitrary and unjustified. But it is felt to be justified. It has become a part of the child's "super-ego," as recent psychology would say; or, in the language of traditional ethics, it has become a demand of his conscience. Because the law given by the father is good, and the child cannot help recognizing this, and therefore because the law is inescapable, the child must hate the father; for he seems to be the cause of the torturing split in the child's soul. That is the situation of man before God. The natural man hates God and regards Him as the enemy, because He represents for man the law which he cannot reach, against which he struggles, and which, at the same time, he must acknowledge as good and true. There is no difference, at this point, between the theist and the atheist. Atheism is only a form of enmity against God, namely, that God Who represents the law, and, with the law, the split and the despair and the meaninglessness of our existence. The atheist as well as the theist hates to be confronted with what he ought to be, with the ultimate meaning and good which he cannot deny and yet which he cannot reach. The atheist gives other names to God, Whom he hates, but he cannot escape Him, any more than he can escape his hatred of Him. This is the reason Paul does not say: "Our own spirit witnesses to us that we are the children of God." Our own spirit only witnesses that we are his enemies!

Always when Christianity speaks of God and of our loving God in our daily life, it should remember that. The majesty of God is challenged, when we make Him the loving Father before we have recognized Him as the condemning law, Whom we hate in the depths of our hearts.

"The Spirit beareth witness with our spirit that we are the children of God." Something new has come, a new reality, a new being, a Spirit distinguished from our spirit, yet able to make itself understood to our spirit, beyond us and yet in us. The whole message of Christianity is contained in this statement. Christianity overcomes law and despair by the certainty that we are the children of God. There is nothing higher than this. For although we are in the flesh and under the law and in the cleavage of our existence, we are, at the same time, in the Spirit and in the fulfillment and unity with the ultimate meaning of our life. This paradox, for Paul, is the astonishing and, humanly speaking, the *incredible* content of Christianity. This certainty gave him the impulse to preach his message to the whole world, and to conquer it. It gave him the power to break with his caste and his nation, and to take upon himself an abundant amount of suffering and struggle, and finally, martyrdom. Christ has overcome the law, the system of commands which makes us slaves because we cannot escape it, and which throws us into despair because it makes us enemies of our own destiny and our own ultimate good. Having this certainty that we are the children of God means, for Paul, "having the Spirit." Out of this certainty follows everything that makes Christian existence what it is. First of all, it gives us the power to cry, "Abba, Father!" that is, the power to pray the Lord's prayer. Only he who has the Spirit has the power to say "Father" to God.

Everybody can *say* the Lord's prayer, and it is recited millions and millions of times every day. But how many of those who say it have received the power to *pray* it?

The fatherhood of God, which is the greatest and most incredible concept of Christianity, has become one of the most usual and insignificant phrases of daily life. Christianity has forgotten that in every invocation of God as Father the enmity against God must be overcome, the ecstatic certainty of our childhood must be given by the Spirit. Many of those outside Christianity know more about it than those within it. They know how paradoxical and impossible it is to call God "Father." But where it happens that man has gained freedom, "the spirit of bondage" to fear is overcome by "the spirit of adoption." When a child has a moment that we could call a moment of grace, he suddenly does the good freely, without command, and more than had been commanded; happiness glows in his face. He is balanced within himself, without enmity, and is full of love. Bondage and fear have disappeared; obedience has ceased to be obedience and has become free inclination; ego and super-ego are united. This is the liberty of the children of God, liberty from the law, and because from the law, also from the condemnation to despair.

Those who have the Spirit walk not after the flesh but after the Spirit. The power of infinite desire and unlimited will to power is broken. It is not extinguished; the hunger and thirst for life remain. But when, for us, the Spirit is present, desire is transformed into love and will to power into justice. In the great chapter on love in First Corinthians, Paul makes it clear that love is the fruit of the Spirit, and that there is no love without the Spirit. Love is not a matter of law. As long as it is commanded, it does not exist. Neither is it a matter of sentimental emotion. It is impossible for the natural man; and it is ecstatic in its appearance, like every gift of the Spirit.

And finally, Spirit is life. "To be carnally minded is death." There is a man of our time who discovered the truth of this profound statement. Sigmund Freud recognized that at the root of our infinite desire lies the will to death. The individual, feeling the impossibility of fulfilling his desire, wants to rid himself of it by losing himself as an individual. Death is inevitable, but it is also chosen. Not only *must* we die, we also *want* to die, "for to be carnally minded is death."

"But," continues Paul, "to be spiritually minded is life." Spirit is life, creative life, as the ancient hymn, *Veni Croator Spiritus*, declares. The word "spirit" has largely disappeared from our daily language and entirely from our scientific terminology. It is replaced by "reason." But reason argues about what it has received; it analyzes life and often kills life. It is not life itself; it is without creative power. But the Spirit is power as well as reason, uniting and transcending them. It is creative life. Neither power alone, nor reason alone, creates the works of art and poetry, of philosophy and politics; the Spirit creates them individually and universally, powerful and full of reason at the same time. In every great human work we admire the inexhaustible depth of its individual and incomparable character, the power of something which happens but once and cannot be repeated and that, nevertheless, is visible to century after century, universal and accessible in every period.

No argument of reason can give certainty. The finite cannot argue for the infinite; it cannot reach God and it can never reach its own eternity. But there are two certainties. One dwells in every soul which knows about itself. It is the certainty which the law imposes that no life and no death, no courage and no flight, can liberate us from the command to be what we ought to be and the impossibility to be so, the condemnation of which is despair. The eternity of despair encompasses us in the moment that we are conscious of our witness to the law. The other certainty dwells in those who have the Spirit; they are beyond their own finiteness and they cannot use arguments, for their eternity is present to them. It is not a matter of a future life after death; it is the convincing presence of the Spirit Who is Life, beyond life and death.

In the story of Pentecost, the Spirit of Christ shows its creativity in both directions, the individual and universal. Each disciple receives the fiery tongue that is the new creative Spirit. Members of all nations, separated by their different tongues, understand each other in this New Spirit, which creates a new peace, beyond the cleavages of Babel—the peace of the Church. Furthermore, for Paul, the Spirit is eternal life. It is obvious that the certainty that we are children of God, that we are united with the eternal meaning of our life, is either itself eternal or is nothing. There is no rational argument for the immortality of our souls. Here and now we are encompassed in the never-ending despair brought on us by the law. Here and now we are encompassed in the eternal and inexhaustible life created by the Spirit, which witnesses to the fact that we are the children of God.

But someone may say: "I have not received this witness. I have not experienced the Spirit of which Paul speaks. I am not Christian in this sense." Listen to Paul's reply. Perhaps it is the most puzzling and mysterious of all his sayings. "Likewise the Spirit also helpeth our infirmities. For we know not what we should pray for as we ought; but the Spirit itself maketh intercession for us with groanings which cannot be uttered; and he that

searcheth the hearts knoweth what is the mind of the
Spirit, because he maketh intercession for the saints
according to the will of God." Paul recognizes the fact
that usually we are possessed by weakness which makes
the experience of the Spirit and the right prayer impossible. But he tells us that in these periods we must not
believe that the Spirit is far from us. It is within us, although not experienced by us. Our sighing in the depth
of our souls, which we are not able to articulate, is taken
by God to be the work of the Spirit within us. To the
man who longs for God and cannot find Him; to the
man who wants to be acknowledged by God and cannot even believe that He is; to the man who is striving
for a new and imperishable meaning of his life and cannot discover it—to this man Paul speaks. We are each
such a man. Just in this situation, where the Spirit is far
from our consciousness, where we are unable to pray
or to experience any meaning in life, the Spirit is working quietly in the depth of our souls. In the moment
when we feel separated from God, meaningless in our
lives, and condemned to despair, we are not left alone.
The Spirit, sighing and longing in us and with us, represents us. It manifests what we really are. In feeling this
against feeling, in believing this against belief, in knowing this against knowledge, we, like Paul, possess all.
Those outside that experience possess nothing. Paul, in
spite of the boldness of his faith and the depth of his
mysticism, is most human, most realistic—nearer to those
who are weak than to those who are strong. He knows
that we, with all other creatures, are in the stage of
expectation, longing and suffering with all animals and
flowers, with the oceans and winds. The soundless
mourning of these other creatures echoes the soundless
longing of the human soul. Paul knows that what we

are to be has not yet appeared. And yet he has written his triumphant and ecstatic letter on Spirit and Life. It is not his spirit which inspired him to write those words, but rather the Spirit which has witnessed to his spirit and which witnesses to our spirits that we are the children of God.

17

HE WHO IS THE CHRIST

And Jesus went out, and his disciples, into the towns of Caesarea Philippi: and by the way he asked his disciples, saying unto them, Whom do men say that I am? And they answered, John the Baptist: but some say, Elias; and others, One of the prophets. And he saith unto them, But whom say ye that I am? And Peter answereth and saith unto him, Thou art the Christ. And he charged them that they should tell no man of him. And he began to teach them, that the Son of man must suffer many things, and be rejected of the elders, and of the chief priests, and scribes, and be killed, and after three days rise again. And he spake that saying openly. And Peter took him, and began to rebuke him. But when he had turned about and looked on his disciples, he rebuked Peter, saying, Get thee behind me, Satan: for thou savourest not the things that be of God, but the things that be of men. MARK 8:27-33.

THIS STORY IS THE CENTRE OF Mark's Gospel. And in this story we find the heart of the Christian message. The message is infinitely simple, yet rich and profound, and concentrated in four words:

141

"Thou art the Christ." Let us think about this message in the light of our story, which is the real beginning of the Passion and Death.

Then Jesus and his disciples set out for the villages of Caesarea and Philippi, on a road between some unimportant villages, at a time which seems indefinite— "then." But on this road occurred the most important event of human history. It is the most important not only from the point of view of the believer, but also from that of the detached observer of world history. And this indefinite "then" pointed to the most definite and decisive moment in the experience of mankind, the moment in which one man dared to say to another: "Thou art the Christ."

On the road, He inquired of His disciples, "Who do people say I am?" "John the Baptist," they told him, "although some say that you are Elijah, and others, that you are one of the prophets." Why did they give Him titles that elevated Him above the ordinary human being? It was because they expected something extraordinary: the coming of the new world order in the near future. All generations of mankind had waited in vain for this new stage of the world, in which justice and peace would reign. The people believed that their generation would witness its coming. But before it would come, forerunners would have to appear, to announce its coming and to prepare the people. Elijah would come from heaven, to which he had been elevated; perhaps Jeremiah would rise from the dead; or some other prophet would appear; even John the Baptist might return from his grave. They felt that behind the figure of this teaching and healing Rabbi some mysterious thing was hidden. They thought that He must be the mask for one of the forerunners, who would come to

prepare the new and final period of history. That is what
the disciples heard from the people.

Although there have been two thousand years of
Christianity, there are still such people. Jesus, for them,
remains the forerunner. The new world and he who is
to bring it in are still to come. Justice and peace have
not yet begun to rule. The new world may be near at
hand, or it may be still far from us. In any case, it has
not appeared. That is the characteristic feeling of the
Jewish people, the feeling that prevents them from
becoming Christian. It is also the feeling of large groups
within present-day Christendom, the feeling that drives
them to wait and to work for the world of peace and
justice, although they are constantly disappointed, and
constantly have to start over again. If Jesus should ask
us today, "Who do people say that I am?" we should
have to answer exactly as His first disciples did: that He
was one of the forerunners, and although perhaps the
greatest of them all, probably not the last one; a forerunner and a prophet, but not he who will fulfill all
things. The reign of justice and peace, the new world,
has not yet come.

And so He inquired of them, "Whom do *you* say that
I am?" That is the question which is put before every
Christian at every time. It is the question which is put
before the Church as a whole, because the Church is
built upon the answer to this question, the reply of
Peter: "Thou art the Christ". Peter did not simply add
another, and more lofty, name to the names given by
the people. Peter said, "Thou art the Christ". In these
words he expressed something which was entirely different from what the people had said. He denied that
Jesus was a forerunner; he denied that somebody else
should be expected. He asserted that the decisive thing

of history had appeared, and that the Christ, the bearer of the new, had come in this man Jesus, Who was walking with him along a dusty village road north of Palestine.

Can we still feel the meaning of Peter's statement? It is hard for us, because the word "Christ" has become the second name for Jesus. But when Peter called Jesus the Christ, the word "Christ" was still a vocational title. It designated Him, Who was to bring the liberation of Israel, the victory of God over the nations, the transformation of the human heart, and the establishment of the Messianic reign of peace and justice. Through the Christ history would be fulfilled. God would again become the Lord of mankind; and the earth would be changed into a place of blessedness. All this was implied in Peter's words, "Thou art the Christ".

The greatness and tragedy of the moment in which Peter uttered these words are visible in the reaction of Jesus: He forbade them to tell anyone about Him. The Messianic character of Jesus was a mystery. It did not mean to Him what it meant to the people. If they had heard Him call Himself the Christ, they would have expected either a great political leader or a divine figure coming from heaven. He did not believe that a political action, the liberation of Israel and the crushing of the Empire, could create a new reality on earth. And He could not call Himself the heavenly Christ without seeming blasphemous to those who, by necessity, misunderstood Him. For Christ is neither the political "king of peace" whom the nations of all history expected, and whom we expect today just as ardently; nor is He the heavenly "king of glory" whom the many visionaries of His day expected, and whom we also expect today. His mystery is more profound; it cannot be expressed through the traditional names. It can only be revealed by the events which were to come after Peter's confession: the suffering, death, and rising again. Perhaps if He should appear today, He would forbid the ministers of the Christian Church to speak of Him for a long time. "He forbade them to tell anyone about Him." Our churches speak of Him day after day, Sunday after Sunday, some more in terms of the political king of peace, some more in terms of the heavenly king of glory. They call Him Jesus Christ, forgetting, and making us forget, what it means to say: Jesus is the Christ. The most incredible and humanly impossible event—a wandering Jewish Rabbi is the Christ—has become natural to us. Let us at least sometimes remind ourselves and our people that *Jesus Christ* means *Jesus Who is said to be the Christ*. Let us ask ourselves and others from time to time whether we can seriously agree with Peter's ecstatic exclamation, whether we are likewise overwhelmed by the mystery of this Man. And if we cannot answer affirmatively should we not at least be silent, in order to preserve the mystery of the words, instead of destroying their meaning by our common talk?

And He proceeded to teach them that the Son of Man must endure much suffering, must be rejected by the elders and the chief priests and the scribes, must be killed, and after three days rise again. He spoke of this quite freely. The moment in which Peter called Him the Christ, Jesus prophesied His suffering and death. He began to reveal the mystery of His Messianic destiny. It was contrary to everything that the people expected, that the visionaries dreamt, and that the disciples hoped for. He was to be rejected by the political authorities of the nation, whose king the Christ was supposed to be. He was to be rejected by the religious authorities of a selected people, whose leader the Christ was supposed to become. He was to be rejected by the cultural authorities of that tradition which was supposed to overcome all pagan tradition through the Christ. *He* was to suffer—He Who was expected to transform all suffering into blessedness. *He* was to die—He Who was supposed to appear in divine glory. Jesus did not deny His Messianic vocation. In the symbolic words concerning the "rising after three days", He indicated that His rejection and His death would not be a defeat, but rather the necessary steps to His becoming the Christ. He was to be the Christ only as a suffering and dying Christ. Only as such *is* He the Christ, or, as He called Himself more mysteriously, the Son of Man.

Peter took Him and began to reprove Him for His words. But Jesus turned to him, and looking at His disciples, rebuked Peter, saying, "Get behind me, you Satan. Your outlook is not God's, but man's." Nobody in Jesus' time would have doubted the fact that God sent suffering and martyrdom even to the righteous. The Old Testament proved that on every page. Therefore, it was not that fact which has made the history of the Passion the most important part of the whole Gospel. It was not the value of suffering and the value of an heroic death, which have given the power to the picture of the Crucified. There have been many pictures of creative suffering and of heroic death in human history. But none of them can be compared with the picture of Jesus' death. Something unique happened in His suffering and death. It was, and is, a divine mystery, humanly unintelligible, divinely necessary. Therefore, when Peter, shocked and overwhelmed by sorrow and love, tried to prevent Him from going to Jerusalem, Jesus considered his pleading a satanic temptation. It would have destroyed His Messianic character. As the Christ, He would have to suffer and die. The real Christ was not the Christ in power and glory.

The Christ had to suffer and die, because whenever the Divine appears in all Its depth, It cannot be endured by men. It must be pushed away by the political powers, the religious authorities, and the bearers of cultural tradition. In the picture of the Crucified, we look at the rejection of the Divine by humanity. We see that, in this rejection, not the lowest, but the highest representatives of mankind are judged. Whenever the Divine appears, It is a radical attack on everything that is good in man, and therefore man must repel It, must push It away, must crucify It. Whenever the Divine manifests Itself as the new reality, It must be rejected by the representatives of the old reality. For the Divine does not complete the human; It revolts against the human. Because of that, the human must defend itself against It, must reject It, and must try to destroy It.

Yet when the Divine is rejected, It takes the rejection upon Itself. It accepts our crucifixion, our pushing away, the defence of ourselves against It. It accepts our refusal to accept, and thus conquers us. That is the centre of the mystery of the Christ. Let us try to imagine a Christ Who would not die, and Who would come in glory to impose upon us His power, His wisdom, His morality, and His piety. He would be able to break our resistance by His strength, by His wonderful government, by His infallible wisdom, and by His irresistible perfection. But He would not be able to win our hearts. He would bring a new law, and would impose it upon us by His all-powerful and all-perfect Personality. His power would break our freedom; His glory would overwhelm us like a burning, blinding sun; our very human-

ity would be swallowed in His Divinity. One of Luther's
most profound insights was that God made Himself
small for us in Christ. In so doing, He left us our freedom and our humanity. He showed us His Heart, so
that our hearts could be won.

When we look at the misery of our world, its evil and
its sin, especially in these days which seem to mark the
end of a world period, we long for divine interference,
so that the world and its daemonic rulers might be overcome. We long for a king of peace within history, or for
a king of glory above history. We long for a Christ of
power. Yet if *He* were to come and transform us and our
world, we should have to pay the *one* price which we
could not pay: we would have to lose our freedom, our
humanity, and our spiritual dignity. Perhaps we should
be happier; but we should also be lower beings, our
present misery, struggle, and despair notwithstanding.
We should be more like blessed animals that men made
in the image of God. Those who dream of a better life
and try to avoid the Cross as a way, and those who hope
for a Christ and attempt to exclude the Crucified, have
no knowledge of the mystery of God and of man.

They are the ones who must consider Jesus as merely
a forerunner. They are the ones who must expect others
with a greater power to transform the world, others with
a greater wisdom to change our hearts. But even the
greatest in power and wisdom could not more fully reveal the Heart of God and the heart of man than the
Crucified has done already. Those things have been revealed once for all. "It is finished." In the face of the
Crucified all the "more" and all the "less", all progress
and all approximation, are meaningless. Therefore, we
can say of Him alone: He is the new reality; He is the
end; He is the Messiah. To the Crucified alone we can
say: "Thou art the Christ".

18

WAITING

*I wait for the Lord, my soul doth wait, and in his
    word do I hope.
My soul waiteth for the Lord more than they that
    watch for the morning:
I say, more than they that watch for the morning.
Let Israel hope in the Lord: for with the Lord
There is mercy, and with him is plenteous redemp-
    tion.* PSALM 130:5-7.

*For we are saved by hope: but hope that is seen is
not hope: for what a man seeth, why doth he yet hope
for? But if we hope for that we see not, then do we
with patience wait for it.* ROMANS 8:24-25.

BOTH THE OLD AND THE NEW TESTAMENTS
describe our existence in relation to God as one of waiting. In the psalmist there is an anxious waiting; in the
apostle there is a patient waiting. Waiting means *not*
having and having at the same time. For we have
not what we wait for; or, as the apostle says, if we hope
for what we do *not* see, we *then* wait for it. The condition of man's relation to God is first of all one of *not* having, *not* seeing, *not* knowing, and *not* grasping. A religion in which that is forgotten, no matter how ecstatic

149

or active or reasonable, replaces God by its own creation of an image of God. Our religious life is characterized more by that kind of creation than anything
else. I think of the theologian who does not wait for
God, because he possesses Him, enclosed within a doctrine. I think of the Biblical student who does not wait
for God, because he possesses Him, enclosed in a book.
I think of the churchman who does not wait for God,
because he possesses Him, enclosed in an institution. I
think of the believer who does not wait for God, because
he possesses Him, enclosed within his own experience.
It is not easy to endure this not having God, this waiting for God. It is not easy to preach Sunday after Sunday without convincing ourselves and others that we
have God and can dispose of Him. It is not easy to pro-
claim God to children and pagans, to sceptics and secu-
larists, and at the same time to make clear to them that
we ourselves do not possess God, that we too wait for
Him. I am convinced that much of the rebellion against
Christianity is due to the overt or veiled claim of the
Christians to possess God, and therefore, also, to the
loss of this element of waiting, so decisive for the
prophets and the apostles. Let us not be deluded into
thinking that, because they speak of waiting, they waited
merely for the end, the judgment and fulfillment of all
things, and not for God Who was to bring that end.
They did not possess God; they waited for Him. For
how can God be possessed? Is God a thing that can be
grasped and known among other things? Is God less
than a human person? We always have to wait for a
human being. Even in the most intimate communion
among human beings, there is an element of *not* having
and *not* knowing, and of waiting. Therefore, since God
is infinitely hidden, free, and incalculable, we must wait

for Him in the most absolute and radical way. He is
God for us just in so far as we do *not* possess Him.
The psalmist says that his whole being waits for the
Lord, indicating that waiting for God is not merely a
part of our relation to God, but rather the condition of
that relation as a whole. We have God through *not*
having Him.

But, although waiting is *not* having, it is also having.
The fact that we wait for something shows that in some
way we already possess it. Waiting anticipates that
which is not yet real. If we wait in hope and patience,
the power of that for which we wait is already effective
within us. He who waits in an ultimate sense is not far
from that for which he waits. He who waits in absolute
seriousness is already grasped by that for which he
waits. He who waits in patience has already received
the power of that for which he waits. He who waits passionately is already an active power himself, the greatest power of transformation in personal and historical
life. We are stronger when we wait than when we possess. When we possess God, we reduce Him to that small
thing we knew and grasped of Him; and we make it an
idol. Only in idol worship can one believe in the possession of God. There is much of this idolatry among
Christians.

But if we know that we do not know Him, and if we
wait for Him to make Himself known to us, we then
really know something of Him, we then are grasped
and known and possessed by Him. It is *then* that we
are believers in our unbelief, and that we are accepted
by Him in spite of our separation from Him.

Let us not forget, however, that waiting is a tremendous tension. It precludes all complacency about having nothing, indifference or cynical contempt towards

those who have something, and indulgence in doubt and despair. Let us not make our pride in possessing nothing a new possession. That is one of the great temptations of our time, for there are few things left which we can claim as possessions. And we surrender to the same temptation when we boast, in our attempt to possess God, that we do not possess Him. The divine answer to such an attempt is utter emptiness. Waiting is not despair. It is the acceptance of our not having, in the power of that which we already have.

Our time is a time of waiting; waiting is its special destiny. And every time is a time of waiting, waiting for the breaking in of eternity. All time runs forward. All time, both in history and in personal life, is expectation. Time itself is waiting, waiting not for another time, but for that which is eternal.

19

YOU ARE ACCEPTED

Moreover the law entered, that the offence might abound. But where sin abounded, grace did much more abound.   ROMANS 5:20.

THESE WORDS OF PAUL SUMMARIZE HIS apostolic experience, his religious message as a whole, and the Christian understanding of life. To discuss these words, or to make them the text of even several sermons, has always seemed impossible to me. I have never dared to use them before. But something has driven me to consider them during the past few months, a desire to give witness to the two facts which appeared to me, in hours of retrospection, as the all-determining facts of our life: the abounding of sin and the greater abounding of grace.

There are few words more strange to most of us than "sin" and "grace." They are strange, just because they are so well-known. During the centuries they have received distorting connotations, and have lost so much of their genuine power that we must seriously ask ourselves whether we should use them at all, or whether we should discard them as useless tools. But there is a mysterious fact about the great words of our religious tradition: they cannot be replaced. All attempts to make substitutions, including those I have tried myself, have failed to convey the reality that was to be expressed;

153

they have led to shallow and impotent talk. There are no substitutes for words like "sin" and "grace". But there *is* a way of rediscovering their meaning, the same way that leads us down into the depth of our human existence. In that depth these words were conceived; and *there* they gained power for all ages; *there* they must be found again by each generation, and by each of us for himself. Let us therefore try to penetrate the deeper levels of our life, in order to see whether we can discover in them the realities of which our text speaks.

Have the men of our time still a feeling of the meaning of sin? Do they, and do we, still realize that sin does *not* mean an immoral act, that "sin" should never be used in the plural, and that not our sins, but rather our *sin* is the great, all-pervading problem of our life? Do we still know that it is arrogant and erroneous to divide men by calling some "sinners" and others "righteous"? For by way of such a division, we can usually discover that we ourselves do not *quite* belong to the "sinners", since we have avoided heavy sins, have made some progress in the control of this or that sin, and have been even humble enough not to call ourselves "righteous". Are we still able to realize that this kind of thinking and feeling about sin is far removed from what the great religious tradition, both within and outside the Bible, has meant when it speaks of sin?

I should like to suggest another word to you, not as a substitute for the word "sin", but as a useful clue in the interpretation of the word "sin": "separation". Separation is an aspect of the experience of everyone. Perhaps the word "sin" has the same root as the word "asunder". In any case, *sin is separation*. To be in the state of sin is to be in the state of separation. And separation is threefold: there is separation among individual lives, separation of a man from himself, and separation of all men from the Ground of Being. This three-fold separation constitutes the state of everything that exists; it is a universal fact; it is the fate of every life. And it is our human fate in a very special sense. For *we* as men know that we are separated. We not only suffer with all other creatures because of the self-destructive consequences of our separation, but also know *why* we suffer. We know that we are estranged from something to which we really belong, and with which we *should* be united. We know that the fate of separation is not merely a natural event like a flash of sudden lightning, but that it is an experience in which we actively participate, in which our whole personality is involved, and that, as fate, it is also *guilt*. Separation which is fate *and* guilt constitutes the meaning of the word "sin". It is *this* which is the state of our entire existence, from its very beginning to its very end. Such separation is prepared in the mother's womb, and before that time, in every preceding generation. It is manifest in the special actions of our conscious life. It reaches beyond our graves into all the succeeding generations. It is our existence itself. *Existence is separation!* Before sin is an act, it is a state.

We can say the same things about grace. For sin and grace are bound to each other. We do not even have a knowledge of sin unless we have already experienced the unity of life, which is grace. And conversely, we could not grasp the meaning of grace without having experienced the separation of life, which is sin. Grace is just as difficult to describe as sin. For some people, grace is the willingness of a divine king and father to forgive over and again the foolishness and weakness of his subjects and children. We must reject such a con-

cept of grace; for it is a merely childish destruction of a
human dignity. For others, grace is a magic power in
the dark places of the soul, but a power without any
significance for practical life, a quickly vanishing and
useless idea. For others, grace is the benevolence that
we may find beside the cruelty and destructiveness in
life. But then, it does not matter whether we say "life
goes on", or whether we say "there is grace in life"; if
grace means no more than this, the word should, and
will, disappear. For other people, grace indicates the
gifts that one has received from nature or society, and
the power to do good things with the help of those
gifts. But grace is more than gifts. In grace something
is overcome; grace occurs "in spite of" something; grace
occurs in spite of separation and estrangement. Grace is
the *re*union of life with life, the *re*conciliation of the
self with itself. Grace is the acceptance of that which
is rejected. Grace transforms fate into a meaningful
destiny; it changes guilt into confidence and courage.
There is something triumphant in the word "grace": in
spite of the abounding of sin grace abounds much more.

And now let us look down into ourselves to discover
there the struggle between separation and reunion, between sin and grace, in our relation to others, in our relation to ourselves, and in our relation to the Ground
and aim of our being. If our souls respond to the description that I intend to give, words like "sin" and "separation", "grace" and "reunion", may have a new meaning
for us. But the words themselves are not important. It
is the response of the deepest levels of our being that
is important. If such a response were to occur among
us this moment, we could say that we have known grace.

Who has not, at some time, been lonely in the midst
of a social event? The feeling of our separation from the

rest of life is most acute when we are surrounded by
it in noise and talk. We realize then much more than
in moments of solitude how strange we are to each
other, how estranged life is from life. Each one of us
draws back into himself. We cannot penetrate the hidden centre of another individual; nor can that individual pass beyond the shroud that covers our own being.
Even the greatest love cannot break through the walls
of the self. Who has not experienced that disillusionment of all great love? If one were to hurl away his self
in complete self-surrender, he would become a nothing,
without form or strength, a self without self, merely an
object of contempt and abuse. Our generation knows
more than the generation of our fathers about the hidden hostility in the ground of our souls. Today we know
much about the profusive aggressiveness in every being.
Today we can confirm what Immanuel Kant, the prophet
of human reason and dignity, was honest enough to
say: there is something in the misfortune of our best
friends which does not displease us. Who amongst us
is dishonest enough to deny that this is true also of him?
Are we not almost always ready to abuse everybody
and everything, although often in a very refined way,
for the pleasure of self-elevation, for an occasion for
boasting, for a moment of lust? To know that we are
ready is to know the meaning of the separation of life
from life, and of "sin abounding".

The most irrevocable expression of the separation of
life from life today is the attitude of social groups within
nations towards each other, and the attitude of nations
themselves towards other nations. The walls of distance,
in time and space, have been removed by technical
progress; but the walls of estrangement between heart
and heart have been incredibly strengthened. The mad-

ness of the German Nazis and the cruelty of the lynching mobs in the South provide too easy an excuse for us to turn our thoughts from our own selves. But let us just consider ourselves and what we feel, when we read, this morning and tonight, that in some sections of Europe all children under the age of three are sick and dying, or that in some sections of Asia millions without homes are freezing and starving to death. The strangeness of life to life is evident in the strange fact that we can know all this, and yet can live today, this morning, tonight, as though we were completely ignorant. And I refer to the most sensitive people amongst us. In both mankind and nature, life is separated from life. Estrangement prevails among all things that live. Sin abounds.

It is important to remember that we are not merely separated from each other. For we are also separated from ourselves. *Man Against Himself* is not merely the title of a book, but rather also indicates the rediscovery of an age-old insight. Man is split within himself. Life moves against itself through aggression, hate, and despair. We are wont to condemn self-love; but what we really mean to condemn is contrary to self-love. It is that mixture of selfishness and self-hate that permanently pursues us, that prevents us from loving others, and that prohibits us from losing ourselves in the love with which we are loved eternally. He who is able to love himself is able to love others also; he who has learned to overcome self-contempt has overcome his contempt for others. But the depth of our separation lies in just the fact that we are not capable of a great and merciful divine love towards ourselves. On the contrary, in each of us there is an instinct of self-destruction, which is as strong as our instinct of self-preservation. In our tendency to abuse and destroy others, there is an open or hidden tendency to abuse and to destroy ourselves. Cruelty towards others is always also cruelty towards ourselves. Nothing is more obvious than the split in both our unconscious life and conscious personality. Without the help of modern psychology, Paul expressed the fact in his famous words, "For I do not do the good I desire, but rather the evil that I do not desire." And then he continued in words that might well be the motto of all depth psychology: "Now if I should do what I do not wish to do, it is not I that do it, but rather sin which dwells within me." The apostle sensed a split between his conscious will and his real will, between himself and something strange within and alien to him. He was estranged from himself; and that estrangement he called "sin". He also called it a strange "law in his limbs", an irresistible compulsion. How often we commit certain acts in perfect consciousness, yet with the shocking sense that we are being controlled by an alien power! That is the experience of the separation of ourselves from ourselves, which is to say "sin," whether or not we like to use that word.

Thus, the state of our whole life is estrangement from others and ourselves, because we are estranged from the Ground of our being, because we are estranged from the origin and aim of our life. And we do not know where we have come from, or where we are going. We are separated from the mystery, the depth, and the greatness of our existence. We hear the voice of that depth; but our ears are closed. We feel that something radical, total, and unconditioned is demanded of us; but we rebel against it, try to escape its urgency, and will not accept its promise.

We cannot escape, however. If that something is the Ground of our being, we are bound to it for all eternity,

just as we are bound to ourselves and to all other life.
We always remain in the power of that from which we
are estranged. That fact brings us to the ultimate depth
of sin: separated and yet bound, estranged and yet be-
longing, destroyed and yet preserved, the state which
is called despair. Despair means that there is no escape.
Despair is "the sickness unto death." But the terrible
thing about the sickness of despair is that we cannot
be released, not even through open or hidden suicide.
For we all know that we are bound eternally and inescapably to the Ground of our being. The abyss of separation is not always visible. But it has become more
visible to our generation than to the preceding generations, because of our feeling of meaninglessness, emptiness, doubt, and cynicism—all expressions of despair, of
our separation from the roots and the meaning of our
life. Sin in its most profound sense, sin, as despair,
abounds amongst us.

"Where sin abounded, grace did much more abound",
says Paul in the same letter in which he describes the
unimaginable power of separation and self-destruction
within society and the individual soul. He does not say
these words because sentimental interests demand a
happy ending for everything tragic. He says them because they describe the most overwhelming and deter-
mining experience of his life. In the picture of Jesus as
the Christ, which appeared to him at the moment of his
greatest separation from other men, from himself and
God, he found himself accepted in spite of his being
rejected. And when he found that he was accepted, he
was able to accept himself and to be reconciled to others.
The moment in which grace struck him and overwhelmed him, he was reunited with that to which he
belonged, and from which he was estranged in utter

strangeness. Do we know what it means to be struck by grace? It does *not* mean that we suddenly believe that God exists, or that Jesus is the Saviour, or that the Bible contains the truth. To believe that something *is,* is almost contrary to the meaning of grace. Furthermore, grace does not mean simply that we are making progress in our moral self-control, in our fight against special faults, and in our relationships to men and to society. Moral progress may be a fruit of grace; but it is not grace itself, and it can even prevent us from receiving grace. For there is too often a graceless acceptance of Christian doctrines and a graceless battle against the structures of evil in our personalities. Such a graceless relation to God may lead us by necessity either to arrogance or to despair. It would be better to refuse God and the Christ and the Bible than to accept Them without grace. For if we accept without grace, we do so in the state of separation, and can only succeed in deepening the separation. We cannot transform our lives, unless we allow them to be transformed by that stroke of grace. It happens; or it does not happen. And certainly it does *not* happen if we try to force it upon ourselves, just as it shall not happen so long as we think, in our self-complacency, that we have no need of it. Grace strikes us when we are in great pain and restlessness. It strikes us when we walk through the dark valley of a meaningless and empty life. It strikes us when we feel that our separation is deeper than usual, because we have violated another life, a life which we loved, or from which we were estranged. It strikes us when our disgust for our own being, our indifference, our weakness, our hostility, and our lack of direction and composure have become intolerable to us. It strikes us when, year after year, the longed for perfection of life does not appear, when the old compulsions reign within us as they have for decades, when despair destroys all joy and courage. Sometimes at that moment a wave of light breaks into our darkness, and it is as though a voice were saying: "You are accepted. *You are accepted,* accepted by that which is greater than you, and the name of which you do not know. Do not ask for the name now; perhaps you will find it later. Do not try to do anything now; perhaps later you will do much. Do not seek for anything; do not perform anything; do not intend anything. *Simply accept the fact that you are accepted!*" If that happens to us, we experience grace. After such an experience we may not be better than before, and we may not believe more than before. But everything is transformed. In that moment, grace conquers sin, and reconciliation bridges the gulf of estrangement. And nothing is demanded of this experience, no religious or moral or intellectual presupposition, nothing but *acceptance.*

In the light of this grace we perceive the power of grace in our relation to others and to ourselves. We experience the grace of being able to look frankly into the eyes of another, the miraculous grace of reunion of life with life. We experience the grace of understanding each other's words. We understand not merely the literal meaning of the words, but also that which lies behind them, even when they are harsh or angry. For even then there is a longing to break through the walls of separation. We experience the grace of being able to accept the life of another, even if it be hostile and harmful to us, for, through grace, we know that it belongs to the same Ground to which we belong, and by which we have been accepted. We experience the grace which is able to overcome the tragic separation of the sexes, of the generations, of the nations, of the races, and even the utter strangeness between man and nature. Sometimes grace appears in all these separations to reunite us with those to whom we belong. For life belongs to life.

And in the light of this grace we perceive the power of grace in our relation to ourselves. We experience moments in which we accept ourselves, because we feel that we have been accepted by that which is greater than we. If only more such moments were given to us! For it is such moments that make us love our life, that make us accept ourselves, not in our goodness and self-complacency, but in our certainty of the eternal meaning of our life. We cannot force ourselves to accept ourselves. We cannot compel anyone to accept himself. But sometimes it happens that we receive the power to say "yes" to ourselves, that peace enters into us and makes us whole, that self-hate and self-contempt disappear, and that our self is reunited with itself. Then we can say that grace has come upon us.

"Sin" and "grace" are strange words; but they are not strange things. We find them whenever we look into ourselves with searching eyes and longing hearts. They determine our life. They abound within us and in all of life. May grace more abound within us!

20

BORN IN THE GRAVE

And when even was come, there came a rich man from Arimathea, named Joseph, who also himself was Jesus' disciple: This man went to Pilate, and asked for the body of Jesus. Then Pilate commanded it to be given up. And Joseph took the body, and wrapped it in a clean linen cloth, and laid it in his own new tomb, which he had hewn out in the rock: and he rolled a great stone to the door of the tomb, and departed. And Mary Magdalene was there, and the other Mary, sitting over against the sepulchre. Now on the morrow, which is the day after the Preparation, the chief priests and the Pharisees were gathered together unto Pilate, saying, Sir, we remember that the deceiver said, while he was yet alive, After three days I rise again. Command therefore that the sepulchre be made sure until the third day, lest haply his disciples come and steal him away, and say unto the people, He is risen from the dead: and the last error will be worse than the first. Pilate said unto them, Ye have a guard: go your way, make it as sure as ye can. So they went, and made the sepulchre sure, sealing the stone, the guard being with them. MATTHEW 27:57-66.

IN THE NUREMBURG WAR-CRIME TRIALS
a witness appeared who had lived for a time in a grave
in a Jewish grave-yard, in Wilna, Poland. It was the only
place he—and many others—could live, when in hiding
after they had escaped the gas chamber. During this
time he wrote poetry, and one of the poems was a description of a birth. In a grave nearby a young woman
gave birth to a boy. The eighty-year-old gravedigger,
wrapped in a linen shroud, assisted. When the new-
born child uttered his first cry, the old man prayed:
"Great God, hast Thou finally sent the Messiah to us?
For who else than the Messiah Himself can be born in
a grave?" But after three days the poet saw the child
sucking his mother's tears because she had no milk
for him.

This story, which surpasses anything the human imagination could have invented, has not only incomparable emotional value, but also tremendous symbolic
power. When I first read it, it occurred to me more
forcefully than ever before that our Christian symbols,
taken from the gospel stories, have lost a great deal of
their power because too often repeated and too super-
ficially used. It has been forgotten that the manger of
Christmas was the expression of utter poverty and dis-
tress before it became the place where the angels appeared and to which the star pointed. And it has been
forgotten that the tomb of Jesus was the end of His
life and of His work *before* it became the place of His
final triumph. We have become insensitive to the infinite tension which is implied in the words of the
Apostles' Creed: "suffered . . . was crucified, dead, and
buried . . . rose again from the dead." We already know,
when we hear the first words, what the ending will be:
"rose again;" and for many people it is no more than

the inevitable "happy ending". The old Jewish grave-digger knew better. For him, the immeasurable tension implicit in the expectation of the Messiah was a reality, appearing in the infinite contrast between the things he saw and the hope he maintained.

The depth of this tension is emphasized by the last part of the story. After three days the child was not elevated to glory; he drank his mother's tears, having nothing else to drink. Probably he died and the hope of the old Jew was frustrated once more, as it had been frustrated innumerable times before. No consolation can be derived from this story; there cannot be a happy ending—and precisely this is the truth about our lives. In a remarkable passage of his book, *Credo*, Karl Barth writes about the word "buried" in the Creed: * "By a man's being buried it is evidently confirmed and sealed —seemingly in his presence, actually already in his absence—that he *has* no longer a present, any more than a future. He has become pure past. He is accessible only to memory, and even that only so long as those who are able and willing to remember him are not themselves buried. And the future toward which all human present is running is just this: to be buried." These words describe exactly the situation in which the pious old Jew prayed: "Great God, hast Thou finally sent the Messiah to us?"

We often hide the seriousness of the "buried" in the Creed, not only for the Christ, but also for ourselves, by imagining that not *we* shall be buried, but only a comparatively unimportant part of us, the physical body. That is not what the Creed implies. It is the same subject, Jesus Christ, of Whom it is said that He suffered and

* Pp. 84–88, Tr. by J. Strathearn McNab.

that He was buried and that He was resurrected. *He was buried,* He—His *whole* personality—was removed from the earth. The same is true of us. *We* shall die, *we* —our *personality,* from which we cannot separate our body as an accidental part—shall be buried.

Only if we take the "buried" in the gospel stories as seriously as this, can we evaluate the Easter stories and can we evaluate the words of the grave-digger, "Who else than the Messiah can be born in a grave?" His question has two aspects. Only the Messiah can bring birth out of death. It is not a natural event. It does not happen every day, but it happens on the day of the Messiah. It is the most surprising, the most profound, and the most paradoxical mystery of existence. Arguments for the immortality of an assumedly better part of us cannot bring life out of the grave. Eternal life is brought about only with the coming of the "new reality", the eon of the Messiah, which, according to *our* faith, has already appeared in Jesus as the Christ.

But there is another side to the assertion that nobody other than the Messiah Himself can be born in a grave, a side which, perhaps, was less conscious to the pious Jew. The Christ *must* be buried in order to be the "Christ", namely, He Who has conquered death. The gospel story we have heard assures us of the real and irrevocable death and burial of Jesus. The women, the high priests, the soldiers, the sealed stone—they are all called by the gospel to witness to the reality of the end. We ought to listen more carefully to these witnesses, to the ones who tell us with triumph or cynicism that He has been buried, that He is removed forever from the earth, that no real traces of Him are left in our world. And we ought also to listen to the others who say, in doubt and despair, "But we trusted that it had been He

Who should have redeemed Israel." It is not hard to
hear both these voices today, in a world where there
are so many places like the Jewish cemetery in Wilna.
It is even possible to hear them in ourselves, for each
of us to hear them in himself.

And, if we hear them, what can we answer? Let us be
clear about this. The answer of Easter is not a necessity.
In reality, there is no inevitable happy ending as there
is in perverted and perverting cinemas. But the answer
of Easter has become possible precisely because the
Christ has been buried. The new life would not really
be *new* life if it did not come from the complete end
of the old life. Otherwise, it would have to be buried
again. But if the new life has come out of the grave,
then the Messiah Himself has appeared.

21

THE DESTRUCTION OF DEATH

Forasmuch then as the children are partakers of flesh and blood, he also himself likewise took part of the same; that through death he might destroy him that had the power of death, that is, the devil; and deliver them who through fear of death were all their lifetime subject to bondage. For verily, he took not on him the nature of angels; but he took on him the seed of Abraham. Wherefore in all things it behoved him to be made like unto his brethren, that he might be a merciful and faithful high priest in things pertaining to God, to make reconciliation for the sins of the people. For in that he himself hath suffered being tempted, he is able to succour them that are tempted. HEBREWS 2:14-18.

THE DARKNESS INTO WHICH THE LIGHT OF Christmas shines is above all the darkness of death. The threat of death, which shadows the whole road of our life, is the dark background of the Advent expectation of mankind. Death is not merely the scissors which cuts the thread of our life, as a famous ancient symbol indicates. It is rather one of those threads which are woven into the design of our existence, from its very beginning to its end. Our having to die is a shaping force through

169

our whole being of body and soul in every moment. The face of every man shows the trace of the presence of death in his life, of his fear of death, of his courage toward death, and of his resignation to death. This frightful presence of death subjects man to bondage and servitude all his life, according to our text. So far as I stand in fear, I stand not in freedom; and I am not free to act as the situation demands, but am bound to act as the pictures and imaginations produced by my fear drive me to act. For fear is, above all, fear of the unknown; and the darkness of the unknown is filled with the images created by fear. This is true even with respect to events on the plane of daily life: the unknown face terrifies the infant; the unknown will of the parent and the teacher creates fear in the child; and all the unknown implications of any situation or new task produce fear, which is the feeling of not being able to handle the situation. All this is true to an absolute degree with respect to death—the absolutely unknown; the darkness in which there is no light at all, and in which even imagination vanishes; that darkness in which all acting and controlling cease, and in which everything which we were is finished; the most necessary and impossible idea at the same time; the real and ultimate object of fear from which all other fears derive their power, that fear that overwhelmed even Christ at Gethsemane.

But we must ask what is the reason for this fear. Are we not finite, limited and unable to imagine or to wish for an infinite continuation of our finiteness? Would that not be more terrible than death? Is there not a feeling within us of fulfillment, of satisfaction, and of weariness with respect to life, as is evident in the words about the Old Testament Patriarchs? Is not the law "dust to

dust" a natural law? But then why is it used as a curse
in the Paradise story? There must be something more
profoundly mysterious about death than the natural
melancholy which accompanies the realization of our
transitoriness. Paul points to it, when he calls death the
wages of sin, and sin, the sting of death. And our text,
as well, speaks of "him that had the power of death,
that is, the devil"—the organized power of sin and evil.
Death, although natural to every finite being, seems at
the same time to stand against nature. But it is man
only who is able to face his death consciously; that belongs to his greatness and dignity. It is that which
enables him to look at his life as a whole, from a definite
beginning to a definite end. It is that which enables him
to ask for the meaning of his life—a question which elevates him above his life, and gives him the feeling of his
eternity. Man's knowledge that he has to die is also
man's knowledge that he is above death. It is man's destiny to be mortal and immortal at the same time. And
now we know what the sting of death is, and why the
devil has the power of death: we have lost our immortality. It is not that we are mortal which creates
the ultimate fear of death, but rather that we have lost
our eternity beyond our natural and inescapable mortality; that we have lost it by sinful separation from
the Eternal; and that we are guilty of this separation.

To be in servitude to the fear of death during our
lifetime means being in servitude to the fear of death
which is nature and guilt at the same time. In the fear
of death, it is not merely the knowledge of our finiteness that is preserved, but also the knowledge of our
infinity, of our being determined for eternity, and of our
having lost eternity. We are slaves of fear, not because
we have to die, but because we deserve to die!

Therefore, salvation is not a magic procedure by which we lose our finiteness. It is rather a judgment which declares that we do not deserve to die, because we are justified—a judgment which is not based on anything that we have done, for then certainly we would not have faith in it. But it is based on something that Eternity itself has done, something that we can hear and see, in the reality of a mortal man who by his own death has conquered him who has the power of death.

If Christmas has any meaning, it has that meaning. Ask yourself, as you listen to the prophecies of Advent and to the stories of Christmas, whether your attitude toward death has changed; whether you are any longer in servitude to the fear of death; and whether you can stand the image of your own death. Do not deceive yourself about the seriousness of death—not death in general, not the death of somebody else, but your own death—by nice arguments for the immortality of the soul. The Christian message is more realistic than those arguments. It knows that we, *really we,* have to die; it is not just a part of us that has to die. And within Christianity there is only one "argument" against death: the forgiveness of sins, and the victory over Him who has the power of death. It speaks of the coming of the Eternal to us, becoming temporal in order to restore our eternity. The whole man is mortal and immortal at the same time: the whole man is temporal and eternal at the same time; the whole man is judged and saved at the same time, because the Eternal took part in flesh and blood and fear of death. That is the message of Christmas.

22

BEHOLD, I AM DOING A NEW THING

Thus says the Lord
Who made a way through the sea,
A path through the mighty waters.

Remember not the former things,
Neither consider the things of old.
Behold, I am doing a new thing,
Even now it is springing to light.
Do you not perceive it?
A way will I make in the wilderness
And rivers in the desert!

ISAIAH 43:16, 18-19.

Let us listen to words of the Old and New Testaments which speak of the new that God makes in life and history.

Behold the days come, saith the Lord,
That I will make a new covenant
With the house of Israel
And with the house of Judah.
Not like the covenant which I made with their
    fathers

173

On the day that I took them by the hand
To bring them out of the land of Egypt;
Which my covenant they brake,
So that I had to reject them.
But this shall be the covenant
That I will make with the house of Israel after those
     days, says the Lord:
I will put my law within them
And write it in their hearts;
And I will be their God
And they shall be my people. . . .
For I will forgive their guilt
And I will remember their sin no more.
                              JEREMIAH 31:31-34.

(Thus says the Lord God:) . . .
I will give them a new heart,
And I will put a new spirit within them.
I will remove their heart of stone
And will give them a heart of flesh.
                              EZEKIEL 11:19.

(Thus says the Lord God:) . . .
I ignore the troubles of the past.
I shut mine eyes to them.
For, behold, I create new heavens and a new earth.
The past shall be forgotten
And never come to mind.
Men shall rejoice forever in what I now create.
                              ISAIAH 65:16, 17.

But let us not omit the tragic words of the Preacher.

Vanity of vanities, says the Preacher,
Vanity of vanities; all is vanity.

What has been is what shall be;
What has gone on is what shall go on;
And there is nothing new under the sun.
Is there a thing of which it is said:
Lo, this is new?
It was already in existence in the ages
Which were before us.
ECCLESIASTES 1:2, 9-10.

And this is the answer the apostle gives:

Therefore if any one is in Christ, he is a new crea-
tion. The old has passed away; behold, all things
have become new.
II CORINTHIANS 5:17.

(And Jesus said to them:) . . . No one puts a piece
of new cloth on an old garment, for the patch tears
away from the garment, and a worse tear is made.
Neither is new wine put into old wineskins; if it is,
the skins burst and the wine is spilled, and the skins
are destroyed; but new wine is put into new wine-
skins, and so both are preserved.
MATTHEW 9:16-17.

And finally, let us listen to the seer of the New Testament:

Then I saw a new heaven and a new earth; for the first heaven and the first earth had passed away. . . . And I saw the holy city, the New Jerusalem, coming down . . . and I heard a great voice from the throne saying: Behold, the dwelling of God is with men . . . he will wipe away every tear from their eyes and death shall be no more, for the former things have passed away. . . . Behold, I make all things new.

REVELATION 21:1-5.

LET US MEDITATE ON THE OLD AND the new, in ourselves and in our world. In these Biblical texts the new is contrasted with the old: the old is rejected, and there is stated, in passionate words, expectation of the new. Even the Preacher, who denies the possibility of anything really new on earth, does not hide his longing for the new, and his disappointment in not being able to find it. Why do these writers feel and speak in this way? Why do they prefer the new to the old, and why do they believe that God is the God of the new? Why do they demand and expect the new birth, the new heart, the new man, the new covenant, the New Jerusalem, the new heaven and the new earth?

They do not announce the new because they believe what many people of the last decades have believed: that the later things are better than the former things simply *because* they are later; that new developments are more divine than old ones, because they are nearer

to a final perfection; that God guarantees a perpetual
progress, and that for *this* reason He is the God of the
new. Against such illusions the disappointed words of
the Preacher are true for all history. And certainly such
illusions are not the content of the prophetic and apostolic preaching concerning the new. What is the content
of their expectation? What do they mean when they
warn us not to consider the things of old? What are
those old things, and what are the new things which
they ask us to see and to accept?

"Old" sometimes means that which lasts through all
times, that which is today as it was in the past and as
it shall be in all the future. There is something that does
not age, something that is always old and always new
at the same time, because it is eternal. God is sometimes
called the "ancient of days" or the "Redeemer of old".
The wisdom of old and the law of God, which are as old
as the foundations of the earth, are praised just because
they are old; nothing new is set against them as no new
God is set against the God of old. "Old" as it is used here
means "everlasting", pointing to that which is not subject to the change of time.

But in the texts we have read from the words of the
unknown prophet of the exile, in the 43rd chapter of
Isaiah, "old" means just the opposite. It means that
which passes away and shall not be remembered any
more—the destiny of everything created, of the stars
as well as of the grass in the field, of men as well as of
animals, of nations as well as of individuals, of the
heavens as well as of the earth. They all become old
and pass away. What does it mean to say that somebody
or something becomes old? All life grows; it desires and
strives to grow, and it lives as long as it grows. Men always have been fascinated by the law of growth. They

have called that which helps growth good, and they
have called that which hinders it evil. But let us look
more deeply into the law of growth and into its tragic
nature. Whether we observe the growth of a living cell
or of a human soul or of a historical period, we see that
growth is gain and loss at the same time; it is both fulfillment and sacrifice. Whatever grows must sacrifice
many possible developments for the one through which
it chooses to grow. He who wants to grow as a scientist
may have to sacrifice poetic or political possibilities
which he would like to develop. He has to pay a price.
He cannot grow equally in all directions. The cells
which adapt themselves to one function of the body
lose the power to adapt themselves to other functions.
Periods of history which are determined by one idea
suppress the truth of other possible ideas. Every decision excludes possibilities and makes our life narrower.
Every decision makes us older and more mature. Youth
is openness. But every decision closes doors. And that
cannot be avoided; it is an inescapable destiny. Life
makes decisions in every moment; life closes doors in
every moment. We proceed from the first minute of our
lives to the last minute, *because* we are growing. The
law of growth lends us greatness, and therefore tragedy.
For the excluded possibilities belong to us; they have a
right of their own. Therefore, they take their vengeance
upon our lives which have excluded them. They may
die; and with them, great powers of life and large re-
sources of creativity. For life, as it grows, becomes a
restricted power, more rigid and inflexible, less able to
adapt itself to new situations and new demands. Or, on
the other hand, the excluded possibilities may *not* die.
They may remain within us, repressed, hidden, and dangerous, prepared to break into the life process, not as a

creative resource, but as a destructive disease. Those
are the two ways in which the aging life drives toward
its own end: the way of self-limitation, and the way of
self-destruction. Often the two ways merge, carrying
death into all realms of life.

Let us consider one of these realms—our historical
situation, the life of our period. Our period has become
what it is through innumerable decisions and, therefore, innumerable exclusions. Some of the excluded possibilities have died away, depriving us of their creative
power. Many of them have not died, and after having
disappeared for a time, are now returning destructively.
The former greatness of our period has produced its
present tragedy and that of all who live within it. Even
those who are young amongst us are old, in so far as
they belong to an aged period. They are young in their
personal vitality; they are old because of their participation in the tragedy of our time. It is an illusion to believe that youth *as youth* has saving power. When the
ancient empires aged and died, their youth did not
save them. And our younger generation will not save
us, simply by virtue of the fact that it is young.

We have made many decisions in order to become
what we are. But every decision is tragic, because it is
the decision against something which cannot be suppressed with impunity.

At the beginning of our period we decided for *freedom*. It was a right decision; it created something new
and great in history. But in that decision we excluded
the security, social and spiritual, without which man
cannot live and grow. And now, in the old age of our
period, the quest to sacrifice freedom for security splits
every nation and the whole world with really daemonic
power. We have decided for *means* to control nature

and society. We have created them, and we have
brought about something new and great in the history
of all mankind. But we have excluded ends. We have
never been ready to answer the question, "For what?"
And now, when we approach old age, the means claim
to be the ends; our tools have become our masters, and
the most powerful of them have become a threat to our
very existence. We have decided for *reason* against out-
grown traditions and honored superstitions. That was
a great and courageous decision, and it gave a new dignity to man. But we have, in that decision, excluded
the soul, the ground and power of life. We have cut off
our mind from our soul; we have suppressed and mis-
treated the soul within us, in other men, and in nature.
And now, when we are old, the forces of the soul break
destructively into our minds, driving us to mental disease and insanity, and effecting the disintegration of the
souls of uncounted millions, especially in this country,
but also all over the world.

From the very beginning of our period we have decided for the *nation,* as the expression of our special
way of life and of our unique contribution to history.
The decision was great and creative, and for centuries
it was effective. But in that decision we excluded mankind and all symbols expressing the unity of all men.
The former unity was broken, and no international
group has been able to re-establish it. Now, in the old
age of our period, the most powerful nations themselves
claim to represent mankind, and try to impose their
ways of life upon all men, producing, therefore, wars
of destruction, which will perhaps unite all mankind
in the peace of the grave.

Our period has decided for a *secular* world. That was
a great and much-needed decision. It threw a church

from her throne, a church which had become a power
of suppression and superstition. It gave consecration and
holiness to our daily life and work. Yet it excluded those
deep things for which religion stands: the feeling for the
inexhaustible mystery of life, the grip of an ultimate
meaning of existence, and the invincible power of an
unconditional devotion. These things *cannot* be excluded. If we try to expel them in their divine images,
they re-emerge in daemonic images. Now, in the old
age of our secular world, we have seen the most horrible
manifestation of these daemonic images; we have looked
more deeply into the mystery of evil than most generations before us; we have seen the unconditional devotion of millions to a satanic image; we feel our period's
sickness unto death.

This is the situation of our world. Each of us should
realize that he participates in it, and that the forces in
his own soul which make him old, often in early years,
are part of the forces which make our period old. Each
of us strengthens these forces, and each of us is a victim
of them at the same time. We are in the desert of which
the prophet speaks, and none among us knows the way
out. Certainly there is no way out in what some idealists
tell us: "Make decisions, but don't exclude anything!
Take the best in *all* possibilities. Combine them. Then
will our period become young again!" No man and no
nation will become young again in that way. The new
does not appear from a collection of the elements of the
old which are still alive. When the new comes the old
must disappear. "Remember not the former things,
neither consider the things of old", says the prophet.
"Behold, all things are become new", says the apostle.
Out of the death of the old the new arises. The new is
created not out of the old, not out of the best of the old,

but out of the *death* of the old. It is not the old which creates the new. That which creates the new is that which is beyond old and beyond new, the Eternal.

"Behold, *I* am doing a new thing, even now it is springing to light. Do you not perceive it?" If the new were a part of the old, the prophet would not ask, "Do you perceive it?" for everybody would see it already. But it is hard to perceive. It is hidden in the profound mystery which veils every creation, birth as well as re-birth. It springs to light—which is to say that it comes out of the darkness of that mystery.

Nothing is more surprising than the rise of the new within ourselves. We do not foresee or observe its growth. We do not try to produce it by the strength of our will, by the power of our emotion, or by the clarity of our intellect. On the contrary, we feel that by trying to produce it we prevent its coming. By trying, we would produce the old in the power of the old, but not the new in the power of the new. The new being is born in us, just when we least believe in it. It appears in re-mote corners of our souls which we have neglected for a long time. It opens up deep levels of our personality which had been shut out by old decisions and old ex-clusions. It shows a way where there was no way before. It liberates us from the tragedy of having to decide and having to exclude, because it is given before any deci-sion. Suddenly we notice it within us! The new which we sought and longed for comes to us in the moment in which we lose hope of ever finding it. That is the first thing we must say about the new: it appears when and where it chooses. We cannot force it, and we cannot calculate it. Readiness is the only condition for it; and readiness means that the former things have become old and that they are driving us into the destruction of our souls just when we are trying most to save what we think can be saved of the old.

It is the same in our historical situation. The birth of the new is just as surprising in history. It may appear in some dark corner of our world. It may appear in a social group where it was least expected. It may appear in the pursuit of activities which seem utterly insignificant. It may appear in the depth of a national catastrophe, if there be in such a situation people who are able to perceive the new of which the prophet speaks. It may appear at the height of a national triumph, if there be a few people who perceive the vanity of which the Preacher speaks. The new in history always comes when people least believe in it. But, certainly, it comes only in the moment when the old becomes visible *as* old and tragic and dying, and when no way out is seen. We live in such a moment; such a moment is *our* situation. We realize this situation in its depth only if we do not continue to say, "We know where the new will come from. It will come from *this* institution or *this* movement, or *this* special class, or *this* nation, or *this* philosophy, or *this* church." None of these, of course, is excluded from being the place where the new will appear. But none of these can guarantee its appearance. All of us who have looked at one of these things as the chosen place of the new have been disappointed. The supposedly new always proves to be the continuation of the old, deepening its destructive conflicts. And so I repeat: the first thing about the new is that we cannot force it and cannot calculate it. All we can do is to be ready for it. We must realize as profoundly as possible that the former things have become old, that they destroy our period just when we try most courageously to preserve the best of it. And we must attempt this realization in our social as well as in our personal life. In no way but the most passionate striving for the new shall we become aware that the old is old and dying. The prophets who looked for the new thing *He* is doing were most passionately and most actively involved in the historical situation of their nation. But they knew that neither they themselves nor any of the old things would bring the new.

"Remember not the former things, neither consider the things of old", says the prophet. That is the second thing we must say about the new: it must break the power of the old, not only in reality, but also in our memory; and one is not possible without the other. Let me say a few words about this most sublime point in the prophetic text and in the experience of every religion. We cannot be born anew if the power of the old is not broken within us; and it is not broken so long as it puts the burden of guilt upon us. Therefore religion, prophetic as well as apostolic, pronounces, above all, forgiveness. Forgiveness means that the old is thrown into the past because the new has come. "Remember not" in the prophetic words does not mean to forget easily. If it meant that, forgiveness would not be necessary. Forgiveness means a throwing out of the old, as remembered *and* real at the same time, by the strength of the new which could never be the saving new if it did not carry with it the authority of forgiveness.

I believe that the situation is the same in our social and historical existence. A new which is not able to throw the old into the past, in remembrance as well as in reality, is not the really new. The really new is able to break the power of old conflicts between man and man, between group and group, in memory and reality. It is able to break the old curses, the results of former guilt, inherited by one generation from another, the guilt between nations, between races, between classes, on old and new continents, these curses by which the guilt of one group, in reality and memory, permanently produces guilt in another group. What power of the new will be great and saving enough to break the curses which have laid waste half of our world? What new thing will have the saving power to break the curse brought by the German nation upon herself before our eyes? "Remember not the former things", says the prophet. That is the second thing which must be said about the new.

"Behold, *I* am doing a new thing." "*I*" points to the source of the really new, to that which is always old and always new, the Eternal. That is the third thing which must be said about the new: it bears the mark of its eternal origin in its face, as it did when Moses came from the mountain with the tablets of the law, opening a new period of history. The really new is that which has in itself eternal power and eternal light. New things arise in every moment, at every place. Nothing is today as it was yesterday. But *this* kind of new is old almost as soon as it appears. It falls under the judgment of the Preacher: "There is no new thing under the sun." Yet sometimes a new thing appears which does not age so easily, which makes life possible again, in both our personal and our historical existence, a saving new, which has the power to appear when we least expect it, and which has the power to throw into the past what is old and burdened with guilt and curse. Its saving power is the power of the Eternal within it. It is new, really new, in the degree to which it is beyond old and new, in the degree to which it is eternal. And it remains new so long as the eternal power of the Eternal is manifest within it, so long as the light of the Eternal shines through it. For that power may become weaker; that light may become darker; and that which was truly a new thing may become old itself. That is the tragedy of human greatness in which something eternal appears.

When the apostles say that Jesus is the Christ, they mean that in Him the new eon which cannot become old is present. Christianity lives through the faith that within it there is the new which is not just another new thing but rather the principle and representation of all the really new in man and history. But it can affirm this only because the Christ deprived Himself of everything which can become old, of all individual and social standing and greatness, experience and power. He surrendered all these in His death and showed in His self-surrender the only new thing which is eternally new: love. "Love never ends," says His greatest apostle. Love is the power of the new in every man and in all history. It cannot age; it removes guilt and curse. It is working even today toward new creation. It is hidden in the darkness of our souls and of our history. But it is not completely hidden to those who are grasped by its reality. "Do you not *perceive* it?" asks the prophet. Do *we* not perceive it?